What a privilege to wa[...]
friends Roy and Shirley[...]
marriage and family life, even with challenges, are not hurt by trusting God. In fact, by going out to help others, our lives are enriched.

Dean Sherman, YWAM Teacher since 1970.

Roy and Shirley are special people with hearts that have been enlarged and softened for others through their own family circumstances. This has been expressed partly through their work to establish the YWAM *inTouch* ministry in Europe to connect with former YWAMers, a blessing for hundreds if not thousands over the years. These Joneses are worth trying to keep up with!

Jeff and Romkje Fountain,
Leaders of YWAM Europe 1989 - 2009 and Founders of
the Schuman Centre for European Studies.

Roy is exceptional! He has the gift of organisation, a sense of duty and an amazing capacity for precision. He is like a delightful blend of the main computer at a Paris Railway Station and one of the Queen's diplomatic personnel, combined with the mechanism of a Swiss watch! Added to all that, he has managed to integrate into his character the sweet smoothness of milk chocolate, the faith of a great leader and the perseverance of a busy ant who doesn't give up.

Roy Jones's absolute must-have quality is his British sense of humour; he seizes every opportunity to make fun of himself. I experienced each of these unique qualities during the fourteen years of his involvement with YWAM

Switzerland, whether communicating with him from a distance or working close-up on joint projects. Whenever we now meet up somewhere on the planet, it's always a cause for fun and celebration.

Olivier Fleury, director of Youth With A Mission Switzerland and founder of 'Jesus Celebration 2033'.

Rachael, our God is able!

Thankyou for serving us in Albania.

Roy   Psalm 92 v 12-15

PERFECT TIMING

ADVENTURES OF FAITH, FAMILY, AND FINANCE

ROY JONES

credo
house publishers

Published by Credo House Publishers, a division of
Credo Communications, LLC, Grand Rapids, Michigan;
www.credohousepublishers.com.

ISBN: 978-1-625860-38-5

Cover and interior design by Frank Gutbrod
Back cover photograph by Ryan Carter

First Edition

"So do not worry, saying, 'What shall we eat?' or 'What shall we drink?' or 'What shall we wear?' For the pagans run after all these things, and your heavenly Father knows that you need them. But seek first his kingdom and his righteousness, and all these things will be given to you as well."
Matthew 6: 31-33.

Contents

Acknowledgements

This is not our story alone. If you have prayed for us, given to our financial support, encouraged and helped us in different practical ways, then it's *your* story too. We may have lived it out — but we couldn't have done it without you. We want to acknowledge and thank you for believing in and standing with us. There are too many to mention here but, as the saying goes: "You know who you are." So do we, and this book is dedicated to every one of you.

Special thanks go to the members of Farnham Baptist Church — our home church since 1990. In particular David Churchill deserves a mention having been involved practically with each of our international relocations. His wife Tricia has graciously helped in the proofreading of this book.

Kevin and Margaret Ashman are wonderful listeners. Several years ago I shared a few personal stories of God's faithfulness to us with them and Kevin suggested that I write a book. Although the final result has had a long gestation period, the seed was planted on that day. Thank you for encouraging me to put my fingers to the keyboard.

I'm also grateful to Janice Cunningham-Rogers who led Writers' Workshops which I set up for her in several European countries. She too inspired me to write as I listened to what she taught. Her wisdom and humour have helped me enormously.

Scott Deaver coached me over Skype from Italy through much of the process. I've appreciated his help in keeping me focused and sticking to deadlines. This has been invaluable. Joey Rauwolf spent many weeks in our home going over the manuscript and his attention to detail has made all the difference. Without Liz Hansford's input from Scotland, this would not be a readable story; she put meat onto the bare bones and brought them to life. Liz passed away before the project was finished; we remember with gladness a life well lived. Philippa Guptara, Linda Panci and Joyce Devereaux, all in Switzerland, gave wise advice and lots of encouragement in the final drafts. For others — not mentioned, nor forgotten — who have helped and encouraged, please know that I'm truly thankful.

The biggest thanks go to Shirley, Catherine and Amy. With God's grace we have attempted to do the possible whilst seeing Him do the impossible. His faithfulness during more than two decades is our testimony. What an adventure it's been, and long may it continue!

Sweden, December 2015.

"Blessed is the man who finds wisdom, the man who gains understanding, for it is more profitable than silver and gains better returns than gold." Proverbs 3:13-14.

Kona Calling

"We'll need time to think about that" was our bemused and none-too-serious reply to the offer from my parents of the trip of a lifetime — a free holiday in Hawai'i. But now, so many years later, how glad we are that we accepted! For it was in Hawai'i that God stepped in and turned our lives upside down.

Shirley and I had married four years previously and everything felt complete. Catherine, at eighteen months old, was a happy, musical child; into everything and a lot of fun to have around. And tucked safely away in Shirley's womb a second baby was on the way. We were content in our lovely home in the village of Crondall nestled in the countryside some forty miles outside of London. We enjoyed attending a church in nearby Farnham, had many friends and life was good.

Things were going well at work too. I'd recently been given a promotion in my Railway job and was now the deputy section leader of a team with British Rail, working on timetables at Waterloo Station for the whole of south-west London and beyond. I even had some responsibilities for the Queen's train when it came onto our region.

Four years earlier, my younger brother Richard gave us the best wedding present we could have dreamt of. We'd escaped from the reception to our new home and just before we lifted our cases to leave for the honeymoon, the door-bell rang. There on the doorstep stood Richard, smiling fit to burst. "I've done it," he said. "Done what?" I asked, fearing some fallout from his drug taking lifestyle. "Become a Christian," he grinned. Words weren't enough. All I could do was hug him and call Shirley to come and hear the good news. I had shared my faith with him many years previously — now he wanted us to be the first to know.

We listened with excitement as Richard started to talk about how he'd been touched by what he had experienced at our wedding. "So, what did you see?" I asked. There had definitely been no water turned into wine. Nothing dra-matic that I knew of; I was puzzled.

"It was your friends," he said. "The way they treat each other. They're loving, kind . . . even respectful. I've not seen that before, anywhere. Especially not among the guys I hang around with."

It was so simple, so unexpected. No witnessing words, no "sharing the gospel." Just the ordinary, everyday way that Christians inadvertently witness through loving each other.

We immediately advised him to join a local church. His new faith could well be a source of ridicule at his job but we encouraged him to stand firm and not to succumb to peer pressure from workmates and friends. Even if they wouldn't acknowledge it in a group setting, they couldn't help but notice the enormous changes which would be taking place in his life.

We honeymooned for a couple of weeks and were out of contact with our family. But when we returned, we did wonder if his miraculous conversion had lasted. He had been so far from God. Could he make such a huge transformation? We need not have concerned ourselves. Not only was Richard attending the church we'd recommended; in his hunger to know more about his new-found Saviour, he went to every event he could — including the Women's Meeting.

It wasn't long before it became obvious to Richard and the rest of us that God had more for him. There was a call on his life. We encouraged him to attend a missions conference in the Netherlands a few months after his conversion. He stopped by the Youth With A Mission (YWAM — pronounced "why-wam") stand in the exhibition hall and the rest is history.

Within several months, he had left his job and was on his way to Australia to study on a YWAM Discipleship Training School (DTS). This is a five to six-month training course of which the first twelve weeks are spent in the classroom focusing on the character, development and transformation of the student. The remainder of the course is a practical outreach phase, usually in a different nation and culture than that of the classroom.

During Richard's DTS outreach to Indonesia, he met and fell in love with Nia, the local leader of another YWAM team. They married a year and a half later and we had the privilege of taking our then-five-month-old Catherine all the way to Jakarta to join in the celebrations.

Shortly after their wedding, Richard and Nia began to study at the largest YWAM training centre in the world, located in Kona, Hawai'i. Hence the very generous offer from my parents of a trip to visit them.

About a month before departing on our dream holiday, two significant things happened. The first was an appointment at the hospital monitoring Shirley's pregnancy where we were informed of a high chance that our new baby would be born handicapped. This rocked our world. We were still reeling from the news when I attended an interview for a very good job with the Channel Tunnel. The tunnel would soon be opened, physically linking Britain and France for the first time since the Ice Age.

I'd previously got within striking distance of another excellent position in the same company and felt strongly that I would have been well qualified to do it. However, at the long interview for that job some two years earlier, the interviewer didn't seem to like the fact I was a Christian. She did her best to trip me up and I fell at the last post. Hard as it was to accept the rejection, in looking back I can clearly see God at work in the process.

The new interview at the Channel Tunnel, just weeks before our departure to Hawai'i, produced the same result. Again, I went through feelings of disappointment and frustration, especially as Shirley and I both had a significant sense that a change of job was on the way. We were unaware that my "career path" would shortly take a sharp turn in a completely unexpected direction. Leaving behind thoughts of work, we packed our cases and set off for the airport.

The long journey to the middle of the Pacific Ocean was straightforward. In spite of traveling nearly eight thousand miles across eleven time zones, we didn't experience much jet lag. Richard and Nia welcomed us with the news that they'd arranged for us to attend morning classes of the YWAM Kona Discipleship Training School. *"That's not the plan,"* I thought. *"I didn't come all the way to Hawai'i to go to church; I want to swim and sunbathe!"* So I played the toddler card and asked what we'd do about Catherine? "No problem," Richard replied "We've arranged a babysitter, she'll be fine." It seemed as if there was no choice.

Unlike me, Shirley was excited at the proposal. She had been keenly interested in YWAM before we met and had hoped she'd join the mission one day. But she put that desire to one side after marrying the man who took the 7:35 train to London each morning to go to his Railway job.

I glanced around the room full of students — some fifty of them in shorts and t-shirts, Bibles in hand. I couldn't help looking at the huge world map that hung on the wall. We were about as far from home as it was possible to be and many of the students were a long way from their countries too. But we were on a different trajectory. Their goal was mission; ours definitely wasn't. This was just a holiday and it would stay that way.

Until going to Hawai'i, I'd heard missionary speakers, given to their needs and "applauded" them from a safe distance. "They" were people set apart who appeared occasionally at special services. Dressed in hand-me-down clothes, they would tell stories about converts and opposition of local witch doctors, unfamiliar food and even more unfamiliar diseases. They wore saintly smiles and always ended every "slide show" with a sunset. An aura of mystery and sometimes even detachment seemed to be about them. Missionaries were definitely not like me. My wrong perceptions were about to be ditched.

An important element of YWAM's DNA is to engage in spiritual warfare. It turned out that this was the subject of the week's teaching at the DTS in Kona. The speaker, Dean Sherman, had been in YWAM for over twenty years; he taught on his theme with authority and sensitivity. Contrary to my previous impressions, I learned that spiritual warfare doesn't mean running around shouting loudly at demons.

In spite of the recent unsuccessful job interview just before we went to Hawai'i, I still presumed that I'd be a railwayman for the rest of my working days. Within a few minutes of Dean starting to speak, I became completely captivated. Suddenly, I wanted to be part of YWAM. It seemed as if the assumption of a future railway career had been cast into the nearby Pacific.

When I told Shirley at the morning coffee break, she could hardly believe her ears. I couldn't entirely work out what was happening either as I listened to Dean's teaching. I'm an administrator, not an evangelist.

For years, all the practical ministries had landed at my feet: Sunday School treasurer, secretary, superintendent and teacher, although I'd felt the least qualified in the latter. Shirley joined me in this work once we were married, but it was clear even then that she had teaching gifts. I'd co-led weekends away for those attending Sunday School and youth groups; latterly we'd hosted a house group for some wonderful young people.

Those experiences with children and youth made me aware of the gifts that God had planted in me. I gained real satisfaction from planning and administering events within the context of our church in Farnham. But. . . doing full-time evangelism in Africa or in a South American jungle? "No thanks!" How could I reconcile the sudden impulse to join YWAM, giving up my hopes, dreams and plans for a successful railway career, with becoming some kind of evangelist?

Fortunately, I didn't have to wait too long for an answer as God is the master scheduler. I'd thought I was pretty skilled at working out the train times on the dense London suburban rail network, but that was nothing compared to the way that God perfectly aligns things. He is the most detailed planner I know, orchestrating events and arranging for us to hear just what we need to — right on time.

Before the next morning's lecture, we went to a worship meeting led by a YWAM staff member from New Zealand. I'll never forget her words: "I feel this morning that we are to ask God for a release of administrators in YWAM."

"Did I hear right?" I whispered to Shirley, sitting next to me with a satisfied grin on her face. Two bolts out of the blue in twenty-four hours? God created me to be an administrator; this just had to be Him speaking. I couldn't wait to hear what the speaker would say next. "This Mission is desperately short of administrators. Let's pray this morning that God will send us some." It was all I could do not to jump up and shout. "I'm one. And I'm going." That was it! So simple, yet so life changing.

We'd received our call to missions in Kona, so we naturally assumed it would be the place where we would serve with YWAM. We were wrong. Hawai'i may be nice to visit for a holiday, but it's a long way from our European home, our families and even from mainland America — two and a half thousand miles to the east. It wasn't somewhere that we wanted to live long-term. Indeed, in some ways it felt as challenging as my previous perception of missionary life: being located in so-called darkest Africa.

The following Sunday morning found us in a nearby church which Richard and Nia attended. The minister got up and announced that he'd just returned from teaching at a YWAM DTS in Salem, Oregon on the mainland. We'd not previously heard of Salem but somehow the name resonated and we wondered if it might be a place of significance in the journey we were about to embark on.

Before leaving Kona we purchased a YWAM book called the *Go Manual*, an annual publication listing details of all the YWAM operating locations and ministries worldwide. Our eyes were drawn to Switzerland and to Lausanne — a city which we both knew. It was the location of the first ever YWAM training school. And guess what? The *Go Manual* section for Lausanne indicated that they needed administrative staff.

Back home in Britain I headed to the office with anticipation. I fully expected to see a memo waiting on my desk asking if any staff wanted to apply for voluntary redundancy. Surely God would fit this piece into place quite easily too. After all, the Railway needed to shrink staff numbers quite often. That was how God would arrange it! I'd worked out in my mind (without the prerequisite of asking Him first) that I'd apply for, and be granted, a payoff from my job. We'd then immediately set sail to do our own DTS and subsequently spend the rest of our days serving YWAM.

But my desk lay empty.

I discretely asked around. No, there were no voluntary redundancies coming up. Impatient to get into YWAM, I wanted God to act fast. However, I was going to have to learn to wait while He taught me the next key lesson of working to His timing and not my own.

After God hit the pause button in the plan, Shirley and I both felt we needed a clear word from Him to confirm that we were on the right path. We didn't merely want to feel peace about the change of direction that our lives were taking; we wanted a word from the Word which we could refer to if life got tough in the future. We waited and watched.

I decided to learn as much as I could about the missionary movement that we now yearned to be a part of and started to read about YWAM on the daily train commute to and from London. One Tuesday evening during my homeward journey, I came across a testimony in a book written by a YWAMer who had served in the Pacific Region. He quoted 1 Chronicles 28:20, *"Be strong and courageous, and do the work. Do not be afraid or dis-*

couraged, for the Lord *God, my God, is with you. He will not fail you or forsake you until all the work for the service of the temple of the* Lord *is finished."*

Arriving home, I couldn't wait to tell Shirley that I had found a great verse of encouragement to share at the Sunday School planning meeting I was to lead later that evening. I quoted it to her and her face lit up. "Don't you see, Roy; this is the verse of confirmation for us to join YWAM too?" Immediately I realised the truth of her words. It stated exactly what we needed to know — that God would indeed be with us as we stepped out of a secure lifestyle into an unknown future.

As I read it to the teachers later on, I experienced deep joy in the realisation of knowing that God could use one verse not only to encourage them, but also to give Shirley and me a promise we could stand firm on. We would be needing this as we were planning to step out of the safety net of receiving a regular salary into trusting God to meet every single need that our growing family would encounter.

Feeling that we now had confirmation of a call to missions, we sent a letter to YWAM Lausanne asking if we could visit. This was in the days before email; every morning we rushed to our letter box in eager anticipation of their reply. When it arrived, the response was that we were welcome to come and meet them but they warned the

YWAM building had temporarily closed. The local authorities were requiring some renovations to bring it up to the standard of current Swiss fire safety regulations. That meant we wouldn't be able to look around the property.

Undaunted, we flew to Paris from where we intended to use our free continental rail travel on the fast train to Switzerland. But the metro line taking us from the airport to the mainline station was not operating, so we had to take a longer, alternative route. Challenges were beginning to pile up. But we were younger in those days; we could face anything! So a heavily pregnant Shirley, Catherine in her buggy and I raced, puffing and panting for the train that would take us to our friend Morag, waiting in Lausanne. We leapt on just in time.

The next day found us happy to be in Switzerland and full of plans to spend many years serving God there. We made our way as instructed to the YWAM centre and, knocking on the door and introducing ourselves, we heard something which left us reeling: "We're now closed indefinitely and probably won't reopen in YWAM's name again." While we were trying to absorb this, the man continued bluntly, hardly pausing for breath: "You've wasted your time by coming here."

What had gone wrong? We were sure that God had directed us to YWAM Lausanne; now the work there no longer existed. We wondered if we'd misheard God and what we had done to make such a mistake. We had been convinced that YWAM would be only too glad to welcome us and the unique contribution we could bring.

During the remaining couple of days of our stay we took long walks by the lakeside, pondering how to make sense of it all. We wondered what our future would hold now. On the return train back to France I remember saying to myself as we crossed the border: *"Will we ever come back to Switzerland again?"* This thought remained once we were back in Crondall. I started to look through the *Go Manual* again. And one place which caught my eye was YWAM Restenäs in Sweden.

However, we didn't have long to think about Scandinavia or any of the many other questions we were asking since we were about to enter the most challenging season of our lives.

This Shouldn't Be Happening to Me

The first Monday of August 1993 had started quietly, but oh how differently it would end. Trains criss-crossed London, half empty as the summer holidays were at their height. I was eagerly anticipating our forthcoming trip to Kona at the end of the month. As I relaxed with a cup of tea at my desk during the mid-morning break, the phone suddenly jolted me to attention.

"The baby," sobbed Shirley. "There's something wrong." It took a moment to make sense of what she was saying, her voice choked with tears. "They want us to go to the hospital at two-thirty. Together."

I felt helpless; a sick feeling rising in my stomach. But I reassured Shirley that it was probably something trivial — or a mistake. As I grabbed my coat to head for home, suddenly it didn't matter whether all the trains across the whole of Britain shuddered to a halt.

Throughout the hour and a half journey I agonised, zigzagging between faith and fear. Why hadn't they told Shirley anything over the phone? No! It would all work out fine; God was looking after our baby. But what necessitated us both coming in? They hadn't done that when we were expecting Catherine. What could they have found out in the blood test which Shirley had been for during the previous week? Why had the nurse not even given a hint about the test results? It was a mistake. Blood tests would be done again and everything would be well.

Shirley sat with Catherine on her lap, snuggling into her for comfort. I put my arms around both of them. This might be the last moment before our world changed. Then we bundled Catherine into the car, dropped her with a relative and headed off for the hospital, two hours early. Distraction. That was the answer. Anything to take our minds off the imminent appointment. So like two zombies we trawled the aisles of the nearby supermarket, mindlessly loading the trolley with stuff we didn't even need.

At the hospital, two-thirty came and went. We sat in the waiting room unable to speak. "Why can't they be on time," I fumed. But once I was in the consultant's room I wished I could be back outside again. I heard him through a fog; words slipping past me.

"Your baby has a chance of having Down's syndrome."

I seized the word "*chance*".

"Just a chance" I said. "Then that's fine. The baby will be OK."

"Mr Jones," he said quietly. "Your baby has a ninety-two percent chance of having Down's syndrome."

"Then our child will be in the eight percent" I thought.

"I suggest an amniocentesis," he went on. "We take a small amount of amniotic fluid from the sac surrounding the foetus. It's done with a fine needle inserted into the uterus guided by ultrasound. It will confirm our diagnosis, though it does have a miniscule chance of error. I need to add that it also involves a small risk of miscarriage. I suggest you go home and reflect for twenty-four hours." We were making our way towards the door when he added: "If it's confirmed, we do offer a termination."

"This is something which happens to other people, not to me" I said to myself, as we got into the car, my mind still charged with emotion. "We'll have the amniocentesis," I announced, turning the ignition key. "That will prove our baby is normal."

"No!" insisted Shirley. "It can cause a miscarriage."

"But the risk is tiny. And we'd feel better."

"No! A definite No. This is our baby. And if something is wrong we'll love it and protect it and we start protecting it now."

In my heart I knew she was right. And with prayer from the leaders of our house group that evening, we made the decision. We would trust the outcome to God. He fathered us. We would father and mother this baby the best way we could. So when we returned to the hospital the next day we said a firm "No".

In the blur of days that followed, we had a high-resolution scan at a London hospital. Once the scan was underway, the operative asked if we already had children.

"Yes, we have a daughter."

"Well it looks as if you'll be having another little girl to join her."

"I think her heart is OK," the operative then reported. "But I can't get her to turn towards me."

"Why do you need that?" I asked.

"Well, she has extra fluid on her neck. And her hands and feet show features consistent with Down's Syndrome. But it's not definite. If I could see her face that would help."

But our baby steadfastly refused to turn her head in the required direction, despite vigorous prodding by the lady doing the scan.

As we left the hospital, disappointed at the lack of any conclusive information, we were determined that since she was first and foremost our child, we would love her whatever might be before us all. If she were to be born handicapped that would be significant — but it wouldn't change the fact that she was ours.

"Let's call her Amy" Shirley suggested. "We need her to have a short name so it's easy. If she does have learning difficulties, it will be less of a challenge for her to write and say."

"*Already we're planning for the worst,*" I muttered. But, once we'd checked, we knew it was the perfect name: Amy means "beloved". And when Shirley prayed and asked God what Amy's middle name ought to be, she sensed it should be "Victoria" which means "overcomer". How right that was too. Amy Victoria needed to overcome all the challenges which might lie ahead.

With five months until Amy's due date, we did our best to get on with our lives, to give our attention to Catherine and make preparations for Amy's birth. We told Catherine that the growing bump in her mummy's tummy would be her new sister. And from then onwards Catherine referred to the bump as "Baybee Aymee".

Amidst the churning thoughts that refused to lie still once we got back from Kona was, how can we become missionaries if we have a handicapped child? We had been called to YWAM and from what we'd seen that would mean travel, challenge and change, mixing with an eager band of boisterous young people who certainly looked as if they wouldn't be quiet on demand. Surely a handicapped child would need stability and a regular routine plus specialist help and extra focus from us and loads of time . . . the list went on and on. How was it all going to fit together? How could I fix it? How could I tie up the terrible tangle of loose ends? And this child who was to bless us began to feel like a lead weight around my neck.

Not once did I ever imagine that one day Amy would have a ministry of her own, that she would break into the hearts of all who met her, that young people would feel at ease with her and that she would meet their needs just as they met hers. What a sane economy God has! He chooses the foolish things of the world to confound the wise — and that included a multitude of lessons I needed to learn.

Shirley understood better than me that God's thoughts are not our thoughts. She was already sure that however Amy turned out, He would include her in whatever plan He had for our missionary lives. She held on to Jeremiah 29:11 *"I know the plans I have for you", declares the* LORD, *"plans to prosper you and not to harm you, plans to give you hope and a future."*

And so together we began to lay some things down — timetabling, fine-tuned planning, personal dreams and expectations. What a sore time that was — but God was tenderly getting us both ready.

Shortly after our return from Hawai'i, Shirley went back to our local hospital for a regular check-up which included another scan. After everything else before, we'd thought this one would be routine, but the operative informed her that she could detect a hole in Amy's heart. Shirley confidently assured her that this could not be the case as the previous high-resolution scan which she'd had in London clearly showed the four chambers of Amy's heart developing normally. We assumed that this operative had made a mistake and thought very little of her comment.

The weeks went by quickly as summer turned to autumn. And apart from the disappointment of our visit to Lausanne, life continued pretty much as normal: work, church, Catherine and pre-natal appointments. Christmas was soon upon us and we enjoyed a lovely break. Amy still wasn't due for a fortnight so we made the most of our time with family.

On New Year's Eve my parents had been due to take Catherine for the day so that Shirley and I could have some time on our own. In the small hours of that morning, Shirley began experiencing strong contractions. Catherine had arrived two weeks late and this train man couldn't comprehend that our second child might come early. So I reassured Shirley that everything was fine, it was probably a false alarm and we — or at least I — rolled over and went back to sleep again.

By the time my parents arrived for Catherine at mid-morning, the contractions were increasing and it was apparent that Amy wasn't going to comply with any human scheduling. Just over two hours later she was born and our lives changed forever. Shirley held her, immediately exclaiming "Look at you — you're beautiful!" Even so, it was evident by her facial features that she did have Down's Syndrome — and all I could think about were broken hopes and dreams.

Within a few minutes, several health professionals had been summoned to the birthing suite. Various checks were made. Looks of concern showed on the faces of some of the medics which we assumed were due to Amy's handicap. I went off to make the usual calls which Dads do; phoning relatives and friends with the good news of our new arrival, but with the bittersweet add-on that our new daughter had Down's Syndrome.

Nearly two years earlier, when Catherine had been born at the same hospital, she and Shirley were placed at the far end of the maternity ward. At the entrance was an incubator which everyone had to walk by. The baby inside was a boy with Down's Syndrome. I remember wondering as I passed it to visit my family, *"What emotions are his parents going through? Sadness, disappointment, maybe even a sense of failure?"* I couldn't have known the answer but felt a deep sense of sympathy each time I saw that incubator — as well as being grateful to God for our own perfectly healthy Catherine.

Now it was my turn to experience all of those emotions, and more. That evening I paid a brief visit to a New Year's Party being hosted by friends close to the hospital but left for home as soon as I could. I didn't feel like celebrating or answering questions. During the night I slept restlessly — seeing the image of our new daughter's Down's shaped head again and again.

Shirley and Amy arrived home on New Year's Day, 1994. But every day we had trips to the hospital for check-ups. Nobody slept well at night; Shirley struggled with the fact that Amy wouldn't suck properly and needed to be fed by a nasogastric tube attached through her nose. The medics watched but didn't say much. We caught nods being passed between them as well as the occasional mention of her heart function. By day four they were clearly concerned; we were sent urgently to the world famous Great Ormond Street Hospital for Children in London to see a heart specialist.

Once again we left Catherine with her grandparents and took our young baby on the first of many train trips to Central London. The consultant explained that Amy's heart didn't have four chambers as it ought to. Instead, her heart had little flaps of skin where the valves should have been. Neither did it have a middle septum (the middle wall of the heart which separates the left and right sides).

We had no idea why Amy's heart defects hadn't been picked up in the high-resolution scan back in the summer. But God knew how much we could carry; being unaware of her faulty heart had enabled us to live through a more peaceful pregnancy than if we had known the truth. God is the God of caring concealment at times. He knows our breaking points and slowly we were beginning to under-stand how lovingly He had chosen to keep things hidden for our protection.

The specialist gently told us that if Amy did not have major surgery on her heart as soon as she was strong enough, we would lose her within the year. With a successful operation, she could look forward to a reasonably healthy life, which could last into her late teens.

We were not prepared for this. Lost in our thoughts, Shirley and I didn't speak much on the train as we returned to collect Catherine. After sharing the difficult news with my parents, we drove home to Crondall. Amy cried continually during the thirty-minute ride, her cry breaking into my self-absorption. All I foresaw was pain and distress, a focus on hospitals and clinics, a sick child who mightn't live long, a wife who could be torn apart emotionally, a toddler who would be abandoned while we attended to her little sister. It all seemed so unfair. What was God doing with our hopes and dreams? "This shouldn't be happening to me," I yelled at Him. "It's too much to bear."

Clearing Skies

Darkness was the worst time; nights when I lay awake with the same relentless record playing in my head. "Nothing's going to be the same again. How can we be in missions with Amy? We're trapped; I'm trapped." Then I would think of Paul in prison, rejoicing in his chains and I'd try to thank God. But the words stuck in my throat. I needed to support Shirley but I couldn't. Every time I escaped to my office in London I felt relief and release, while she was left at home dealing with the everyday realities. I knew Shirley was handling this better than me. And that thought didn't help. Now I had guilt as well as resentment.

But Amy's nights were deathly quiet. She lay silently in her cot with scarcely a whimper and even during the day she hardly ever cried. Sometimes it almost didn't feel like we had a baby in the house. What we didn't know until much later was that she was simply struggling to survive. She was too weak to cry or feed and often went into heart failure.

Unaware of this, we focused on getting used to the regular dashes to our local hospital to have her nasogastric tube reinserted after a curious child at church had pulled it out. And slowly, so slowly, she began to gain weight and we breathed a collective sigh of relief.

In those early days God spoke to Shirley from Isaiah 45: *"Shall the clay say to him who forms it, 'What are you making?' Or shall your handiwork say, 'He has no hands'? Woe to him who says to his father, 'What are you begetting?' Or to the woman, 'What have you brought forth?'"* Verses 6 and 7 are a reminder that *"I am the LORD, there is no other; I form light and create darkness. I make peace and create calamity. I, the LORD, do all of these things."*

We were incredibly blessed with supportive friends who rallied around us. But we watched others struggling to know what to say to us. What *do* you say to those who are going through such profound challenges? We found the most encouraging words spoken to us were simple phrases such as "We're praying for you" or "God bless you."

But the sobering reality of Amy's upcoming heart operation made us stop and think. What if we only had her to care for, to hold and love for just another few weeks? Shirley was especially worried about losing her. The most important thing was to show our gratitude for Amy, so we decided to have a dedication service in case she didn't make it through. This would be an occasion for us to stand before our family and church friends, acknowledging God's goodness in giving us Amy, to thank Him for her and for His love which had held us together. We'd also promise to the best of our abilities, and with God's help, to bring up Amy — however short or long her life was to be — to know Jesus as her Lord and her friend. So at eight weeks old, our special child was dedicated to Him.

The next important date was her life or death operation. We travelled regularly to Great Ormond Street waiting for that moment — the day when she would be declared strong enough for heart surgery. Finally, at just under twelve weeks, she was ready to face the delicate operation to reconstruct her tiny heart.

The day before surgery we checked in at Great Ormond Street. Shirley settled herself into one of the small family rooms so she could be there around the clock. Catherine and I moved into my parents' home which was closer to London than our own house. This shortened my daily commute to work and to the hospital so that I could also give extra time to Catherine during a disruptive time in her young life.

As we stepped into the surgeon's consulting room, his face looked serious. Without formality he looked directly at us. "I need to remind you of the risks of what we are about to do. One in ten children pass away during this kind of surgery and another ten per cent die from complications afterwards. Is that clear to both of you?"

"Yes," I mumbled, trying to put what he'd just said to the back of my mind. What choice did we have? So we signed the necessary paperwork to allow them to operate on Amy.

We'd been told to return in about five hours. To pass the time we wandered the streets of London, doing our best to be tourists but praying as we went. That we felt at peace was miraculous; we just knew it was because Farnham Baptist Church had opened its doors for the morning so that anyone who wanted could go in and pray for a successful operation. We are certain that those prayers carried Amy — and us — through.

Returning on time, we were told that the operation was going slower than planned. I could feel my mouth go dry and my heart start to race. Why was it taking longer? Had something gone wrong? Another hour ticked by and we sat in silence, almost beyond prayer.

When the surgeon came in, we held our breath.

"Everything's gone really well — that was the best operation I've ever performed!" he exclaimed. And I could feel Shirley relax beside me.

"You can go and see Amy now. Don't forget she'll be unconscious and we'll keep her that way for quite a while."

Amy's tiny body was criss-crossed with wires leading to various monitors. She looked so vulnerable and helpless. As Shirley held her tiny hand and stroked her arm, we thanked God for her life and for all that she would become. I made my way to the Railway station in a daze of relief and joy, exhausted by the tension and emotion we had experienced, and started to think about Catherine back with my parents.

Given what Amy had been through, initial progress was satisfactory but fairly slow. Gradually we began to feel institutionalised with Shirley staying at the hospital most nights while I visited every lunchtime and evening. Catherine came to the hospital with me at weekends to visit her sister and mummy even though she was really too young to understand what was going on. I was grateful that my Railway employers were so flexible during this challenging time.

Amy shared the intensive care ward with a few other children. And we watched the lives of other little ones hang in the balance. When a child became well enough to leave the ward we all rejoiced, but if one didn't make it through we all grieved. We saw one twin die from meningitis and other children on the ward were fighting off the same illness.

We learned to read the various monitors which Amy was connected to and began to notice a pattern. Shortly after patients with meningitis were admitted to the ward, Amy's sats (the saturation of oxygen that her blood was absorbing) started to decrease. She had pulmonary hypertension as a complication from her operation and wasn't absorbing sufficient oxygen into her bloodstream to keep her alive. So we began to wonder if she too had contracted meningitis and, more seriously, if she was going to over-come the setbacks. After all she'd been through, would we have to watch her slip away? This was a new and unex-pected blow.

A doctor came to the ward with an offer to test Amy for meningitis. He also suggested that Amy be given a new drug to increase the level of oxygen absorbed into her bloodstream. He warned that the drug hadn't been fully tested but told us he didn't expect any harmful side effects. We readily agreed to anything which might save her life

We had to wait twenty-four hours for the test result. More urgent prayer was needed. So, as quickly as I could, I got on the phone again, this time to Stuart, our pastor. He started to ring others, mobilising prayer support. Among those was Don, the youth pastor who, with his wife Gill, was at that moment hosting a meal for a group of young people. As soon as they finished eating they too joined in the prayer effort to save our daughter's life.

With this unexpected threat to Amy, I suddenly broke. In a rush of emotions, I realised how much I wanted our little girl. I loved her more than my own life, I loved her more than any ministry, more than YWAM, more than any human success. And there, in the small hospital room which had become Shirley's temporary home, all of the selfish thoughts I'd had since Amy's birth dissolved as I broke down in tears. Shirley and I prayed together, calling out to God to save our Amy before I caught the train back to Catherine and my parents.

Shirley returned to the ward. As she stood looking at Amy, three doctors came to the bedside. They silently stared at the monitors on which Amy's vital statistics showed that she was critically ill. One of the doctors looked Shirley in the eyes and warned, "There is nothing more we can do for your daughter, we've done all that we can — it's up to her to fight now."

Shirley remembers wondering "Is this your diagnosis, Lord? What about the promises You gave us when she was in the womb and during her first weeks of life?" Emotionally exhausted she quickly fell into a deep sleep on the chair beside Amy's cot. She found herself walking hand in hand in a white landscape with Amy who was by now about three years old. They were happily chatting when she spotted two large gates in the distance. As they got closer, Amy noticed the gates, let go of her Mum and started running towards them. Shirley called her, "Amy, come back to Mummy." Amy didn't respond — she kept racing ahead until reaching the gates where she rang a bell. Shirley wondered how she knew that the bell was there.

Someone approached the gate from the other side. Amy became animated, as if the person was familiar to her. When the gate opened a man's voice gently asked, "Amy, what are you doing here?" She threw her arms around his legs, pushing as if she was determined to go inside with him. It was clear to Shirley that the two of them knew each other. She quickly recognised the identity of the person and what was happening.

Frantically she called, "Amy, come back to Mummy now." She discerned that if Amy went through the gates she would never return. Looking at Shirley with the kindest eyes and tenderest smile she had ever seen, the man bent down to Amy's eye level and said, "Amy, you need to stay with your Mummy, it's not time." Standing up, he said, "I'll see you later, go back now." With relief Shirley grabbed Amy's hand, and together, they turned around and left.

Awakening from her dream Shirley knew that she needed to call Amy back to life. There in the ward she used her nursing knowledge to pray that every organ, bone, muscle and nerve in Amy's body would begin to function normally. Seeing how distressed Shirley was, a doctor came over offering to get a sedative so that she could sleep. It was only then that Shirley realised that she'd been praying loudly! She told the doctor that she didn't need anything except for God to save our daughter's life. She kept praying until she had completed the job — once every part of Amy's body had been covered.

By the time the three doctors came to check on Amy's monitors her vital statistics were starting to return to normal. The doctor who had spoken earlier told my weary wife that it looked as if our daughter was starting to get through her crisis. Shirley returned to her room where she slept well in the knowledge that the battle for Amy's life had been won.

We still had to wait for the meningitis test result. Those twenty-four hours were the longest of our lives; as per the pattern we were now becoming used to, we actually had to wait a bit longer than the timeframe we'd been given. But the result was worth it, Amy didn't have meningitis. Plus, her oxygen absorption was increasing, the drugs were working! True to her middle name, Amy had overcome these trials. We gave thanks to God. It felt as if we'd turned a corner and it wasn't just with Amy.

My brother Richard sent news to the hospital ward from Kona that Loren Cunningham — the founder of YWAM — would be returning to Lausanne where he'd established the original training centre a quarter of a century earlier. He intended to spearhead the reconstruction and reopening of the YWAM building that had closed by the time of our disappointing visit a few months previously. Richard also mentioned that the team coming with Loren from Hawai'i would be looking for new staff to join them.

Our spirits quickened as we took in this news. Was Amy's improvement connected with this? Had we been correct in hearing God speak to us about Lausanne after all?

Learning to Fly

With an eye still on a future in YWAM, I kept busy on the Railway. I was involved in some minor projects connected with the rail links for the thirty-mile-long Channel Tunnel which by now was nearing completion. Once it opened, trains named "Eurostar," nearly a quarter of a mile long and capable of carrying seven hundred and fifty passengers (more than two jumbo-jet loads), would be arriving at London's Waterloo Station all day long from both Paris and Brussels.

One event on the last day of May which I really enjoyed was an exercise at the new Waterloo International Terminal. Railway staff were asked to help with a safety assessment for the Eurostar trains. The authorities wanted to know how long it would take for a fully loaded train to be evacuated in the event of an emergency. As a thank you, the names of everyone who participated were entered into a draw for a certain number of free tickets for a two-person trip to Paris and back.

At the onset of summer, we decided to book a holiday at a caravan park in the south of France during September which would give us something to look forward to. We reserved a place on the car ferry for several days before we needed to arrive at our destination. Knowing that it was so far to drive in one go to the shores of the Mediterranean, we asked Morag in Lausanne if we could stop off en route with her. She replied immediately that the four of us would be welcome to stay.

Despite the disappointment of our previous visit to Lausanne, it was good to be back. Since Morag was at work in the daytime, we had many hours to ourselves. I wanted to visit YWAM Lausanne which was open again and undergoing renovations. Shirley wisely suggested that rather than turning up unannounced, we should at least phone and ask if it would be possible to pop in. A little apprehensively we rang.

The person who answered the phone asked a few questions before requesting that we ring back in a few minutes. On doing so, we received an invitation to come to the YWAM centre at 4:30 that same afternoon because Loren Cunningham — who by now had relocated to Switzerland — said that he would like to meet us. Our small amount of apprehension suddenly grew larger since we hadn't imagined this scenario.

Arriving at the appointed hour, we were shown around the shell of the building; looking upwards there was no roof, just a bright blue sky! We had a good chat with Loren who made us feel at ease by asking about our-selves and why we'd felt called to Lausanne. Some months later we found out that the day before our visit the staff had been specifically praying for new personnel to come and join them. Loren encouraged us to apply to which-ever Discipleship Training School (DTS) we'd set our hearts on doing and to keep YWAM Lausanne informed of our progress.

We drove away with the realisation that our dream to become YWAMers could now be turning into reality. The remainder of our holiday provided the relaxation that we needed. We spent quite a bit of time talking and praying about a future in the mission and sensed that we should study on a DTS at YWAM Salem in the US State of Oregon. There were several reasons for this: we knew that they ran a parallel children's programme so our girls would be well taken care of while we were in our classes. They also had a focus on Eastern Europe, a region dear to our hearts. There was a good chance that the practical outreach phase fol-lowing the twelve-week classroom part of the DTS would take place there.

The course offered in Salem was called a Crossroads DTS. It was aimed at those slightly older, at a turning point in their lives and looking for a new challenge or, like our-selves, being called into missions after working in a regular career for some years. We had wanted to do our DTS in a cross-cultural setting; going to the USA fitted that particu-lar bill. So, while we were still enjoying the sun in the south of France, we contacted YWAM Salem, asking them to fax the DTS application forms to the caravan site reception.

Once back home, we set about completing those forms. They required several references — including one from my employer. This was a challenge as I hadn't informed the Railway that I was thinking of leaving. Fortunately, one of the managers and I had a trusting professional relationship. He was glad to give me a good reference without mentioning it to anyone else. The applications were duly posted to Salem and we tried to wait patiently for a response.

Meanwhile, the international railway project was gathering pace. More and more Eurostar trains were being delivered from the manufacturers. In the run-up to them being available to the public, rail staff were offered the opportunity of a day trip to test all aspects of the projected service, including a meal service in first class. For me this really was a dream come true.

The staff from our office headed off to Brussels where we had a great day out. On the return trip I was chatting over the meal with Jeremy, a Junior Manager, about major organisational changes taking place imminently on the Railway. This would involve some voluntary redundancies; I indicated that I would be willing to consider leaving for a payoff (without mentioning that the funds would be used to pay for our DTS in YWAM, should we be accepted).

However, Jeremy said that the Railway was pleased with my work so the chances of my being a candidate for redundancy were not high. Although he subsequently mentioned it to our Senior Manager, I was kept in the dark and was none the wiser.

In early December we came home after a day out to find the acceptance letter from YWAM Salem on our doormat. We were to study on the DTS starting in mid-June 1995. From this point onwards, our lives would take a completely different direction. For a start, once I'd left the Railway we'd no longer have a regular salary. We had some savings which we'd built up for a 'rainy day'. It wasn't a fortune, but it would have sufficed to cover our airfares and training in Salem with a little bit left over. I imagined that if I couldn't persuade my employer to make me redundant we'd have to make a large dip into those savings. Since I wasn't yet ready to let go of financial security I was reluctant to do this, wanting to have some kind of "cushion" in the bank. Were we to use the savings now, the cushion afterwards would be very small indeed.

Over Christmas and into the New Year I wrestled with God over this new aspect of "living by faith". In retrospect I realised He was asking me to put my confidence in Him, not because He wanted to test me but to show that He really can be trusted. As January 1995 continued with no apparent sign that I'd be offered redundancy, I eventually prayed, *"OK God, if you're calling our family into YWAM and there's no other way to pay for it, I will resign; we'll use our savings and trust You for the future.*" Shirley agreed and we both felt at peace.

The very next day, I was surprised at work to be asked to go to the Senior Manager's office. "I hear you'd be interested in leaving us?" he questioned me. Having come to the conclusion that I wouldn't need to resign my post until sometime in April, I had said nothing about YWAM at work. "Yes," came my reply, "I would."

He informed me that the government was looking for deeper cuts in Railway personnel numbers than had originally been assumed. If I wanted to leave with a redundancy payment I could do so. He told me he'd see me again in a few days' time when I'd be given my finishing date and details of the payoff.

From that conversation I couldn't guess when my last day at work might be. If the Railway decided that it was going to be sometime after the DTS had started, I'd still have needed to resign and wouldn't get a payoff. Imagine my relief when my manager called me back to sign the agreement. Written in black and white awaiting my signature: the last day of my Railway service would to be in the middle of April — some six weeks before our departure to Salem. It was perfect as it gave us time to get our home ready to leave for the duration of our DTS, to pack and get our affairs in order. Resignation wouldn't be necessary. The agreed payoff was sufficient for all we needed to complete our training in the classroom as well as for the outreach — which we'd heard was to be in Romania. This would be another dream come true as we'd long desired to minister in that nation.

As a further indication that our God was with us, we found out we'd won free tickets on Eurostar in the draw for those who'd taken part in the exercise at Waterloo Station the previous May. One Sunday morning at church we were met at the door by a beaming member of the congregation, Glenys Wilkinson, whose son Robert happened to work for Eurostar. Robert had told his mum and she was delighted to pass on the good news of our win. Just before I finished working on the Railway we used our free tickets to visit YWAM Lausanne so that we could discuss our future with them.

A month after my last day at British Rail, we experienced another example of God's faithfulness and dependability. Shirley slept lightly that night. She knew that instead of being able to count on a good salary transfer into our bank account the next day, we were due to receive nothing. She was naturally concerned about how we would manage once the redundancy money was all gone. The following morning, we received our first ever support cheque in the post. It came from one of Shirley's close friends in Northern Ireland. This was a complete surprise as well as a very real encouragement. It helped us to realise yet again that our God is able. He knows our needs and is completely dependable.

One potential cloud on the horizon was health issues for both Amy and Shirley. Amy's well-being had continued to improve but we still had to take her often to our local Doctor's surgery during the year after her operation. As part of the application process for DTS, we had to have a comprehensive medical check. Shirley's showed an enlarged ovary. A scan revealed a solid lump of "unknown origin". The Doctor was unable to tell if it was malignant or benign but there wasn't time for a biopsy before our imminent departure. She promised to have one as soon as we returned.

Our family left for DTS with great excitement. We were met at Portland Airport by one of the YWAM staff who drove us the fifty miles to Salem. We were the first of the students to arrive but the others soon joined us. Our class consisted of eighteen in total, most of them from the USA.

The first song we sang in YWAM was new to us but it seemed appropriate at the start of our adventure:

> *Oh God you are my God,*
> *and I will ever praise you.*
> *I will seek you in the morning,*
> *I will learn to walk in your ways,*
> *Step by step you lead me,*
> *and I will follow you all my days.*

We got the cross-cultural experience which we'd desired and it was very positive. We were eager to learn and grow in our faith and were helped in this by a broad range of topics in the classroom.

One particular speaker had a gift of healing. Shirley was prayed for and felt the pain leave her ovary. We did have health insurance for the US but in the event, we didn't need to claim on it at all. Throughout our time there Amy was in excellent health which helped us to focus on the DTS.

Another new experience of living a life of dependence on God for provision came when we were invited to visit some friends I'd known since I was a teenager. They lived about eight hours drive from Salem. We had planned to do this over a weekend, but quickly realised that although driving was a relatively cheap option, we wouldn't get there until very late on the Friday night. We could have expected to be pretty tired on Saturday and then we'd have a long drive back to Salem on Sunday. Hardly a relaxing weekend, and not really fair on our hosts either.

We looked into flying and found that although ticket prices would cost quite a bit more, at least we only needed to pay for three of us as Amy — at less than two years old — could travel free. We were a little hesitant but nevertheless felt that we should pursue this.

We booked the tickets and enjoyed a relaxing weekend with our friends. After lunch on the last day, they spent some time sharing issues that had been concerning them. We were glad to provide listening ears, something that wouldn't have been possible had we needed to leave several hours earlier to drive to Salem. Instead we flew back that evening, arriving refreshed and ready for the next week's studies.

When the time came for the outreach phase, Shirley and our girls returned home to Crondall and I went on to Romania. We'd been advised not to take Amy for the whole outreach during the autumn in case she became sick and unable to get the necessary treatment. We were apart for five weeks. Shirley visited the hospital during this time to have a laparoscopy performed on the lump on her ovary. They couldn't find it — the lump was gone!

The three of them came to visit me and the rest of our team in Romania during week six of the outreach. We were all more than ready to be reunited. By this stage the DTS was rapidly drawing to a close. The final part of our training was a week of debriefing and closure back in Salem. During the graduation ceremony I experienced a real sadness of leaving our fellow students. I couldn't help wondering if we'd ever be able to afford to return to North America or if I'd ever see any of these special friends again. I need not have concerned myself. I was to continue learning that God's ways are so much higher than ours.

On The Move

"God's timing is always perfect." We had to keep reminding ourselves of that as the months since we'd heard God's call to YWAM Switzerland became three and a half years. And when you're almost forty, that seems like forever.

We visited YWAM Lausanne a few weeks after the end of our DTS to start the process of applying for a work permit. This should normally have taken two to three months (especially for a European national) but the weeks seemed to drag by as we heard nothing. Boy, were we learning patience!

Initially we'd planned our move to Switzerland for the summer of 1996. With no sign of my work permit being granted and our home to prepare for renting out, plus all the myriad logistics of moving a family, we knew we'd have to delay. So we found ourselves learning to wait until after Christmas.

So, what does a restless individual do while waiting for God to move? Answer: He starts to look at how God wants him to use the intervening time.

God began to draw my attention to the major out-reach in Atlanta that YWAM would be running during the Olympics in July. Without knowing anything of this, a friend offered me a large quantity of his air miles; now I had the means to go. I was learning to see how God directs and connects; learning to keep watching out for Him in action and how I should cooperate. Right away, I got in touch with the YWAM team organising this event and was given a warm invitation to go and help.

So, within a few weeks, I was on my way back across the Atlantic, this time as a fully-fledged YWAM worker. Nearly three years after we had first felt called to join the mission, I was now an active YWAMer! And God had dovetailed my experience and a real team need. With a huge crew and an array of teachers and trainers arriving to speak to the outreach participants, someone was needed to coordinate the arrivals and departures of speakers at Atlanta Airport. What more could a Railway scheduler ask for? It was a match made in heaven!

As well as doing the actual timetabling, I often found myself driving around Atlanta, ferrying speakers to a variety of Christian homes in the area. And God used those "taxi" rides to weave together a tapestry of relation-ships that is still bearing fruit some two decades later.

One of the most strategic of my tasks was chauffeuring for Loren Cunningham and his wife Darlene. I took Loren to several meetings and other appointments which gave us quality time together. Sometimes I felt like pinching myself as a reminder that this was really happening. We'd been in YWAM for just a year and here I was driving the Founder of the mission around. I quickly learned that YWAM isn't hierarchical. Loren and Darlene were down-to-earth and I enjoyed our interaction.

Once the Olympics had started and the YWAM outreach participants had completed their training, my job was over. All too soon it was time to return to the UK, but not before spending time with some of our former fellow DTS students from Salem who had driven right across the USA to be part of the Games outreach. Considering that just a few months earlier I'd wondered if I'd ever go to America again, much less meet any of our classmates, I was truly blessed.

Even though our family's move to Lausanne had been delayed, I went back and forth to Switzerland that autumn to sort out practical things. It wasn't easy for Shirley to be left behind with our two small children and we were both starting to feel the pressure of the impending move. How would we ever get everything finished in time, with our home ready to be rented out? But during one of my absences, friends from Farnham Baptist Church appeared with paint brushes and wallpaper and did a 'Weekend Makeover' on one of our bedrooms. In fact, God sent many people to bless us while we prepared to move. Suddenly we were aware that missionary work is teamwork, with those who stay at home being every bit as important as those who go.

During another Lausanne trip, God put some more of the pieces into place. He made sure I was sharing an office with Andy who'd been Loren Cunningham's Scheduling Assistant for the previous twelve years.

I felt my heart start to beat a little faster one morning over coffee as Andy said," I'm planning on leaving YWAM soon and heading back to the States. There's a vacancy with a Senator in Washington DC and I just feel God calling me there."

"Um, so there'd be an opening here?" I muttered.

"Sure."

"It's just that I worked with railway timetables back in Britain. So I could do that job. Do you think . . ."

"Wow, I'll talk with Loren and we'll get praying."

How amazing that God had already scheduled me to drive Loren around Atlanta where he'd got to know me a little and would know whether we'd work well together as a team.

Within a few days of getting back to Crondall, Loren emailed me with an invitation to become his new Scheduling Assistant. I was over the moon; in less than two years I had gone from working with the Queen of England's train to organising plane trips for the President of YWAM! So, on my next Lausanne trip with a van-load of our things, I spent every available minute learning as much as I could about my new job.

Our last Christmas living in England was unique. We were surrounded by banana boxes, but had a sense of excitement for the future. A new co-worker of ours from Loren's office, Patricia Cook, came over to spend Christmas with us and to help with packing. Our minds were all over the place but we were as ready to go as we'd ever be.

Before leaving for our new life, Farnham Baptist Church held a service where we were prayed for and commissioned as missionaries sent to YWAM. We felt encouraged by the love and support of the fellowship. Early in 1997, we said our goodbyes to friends, bade farewell to our empty house and crammed what we could into the car.

After many ups and downs, and more than three years after hearing God's call in Kona, we finally arrived in Lausanne, our new home. Our family was allocated two rooms in a large YWAM house a twenty-minute walk from the main YWAM centre. This was to be a temporary home as we planned to rent a flat as soon as we could find somewhere suitable. We visited several potential properties but nothing seemed to fit our needs. Even people that we didn't know were searching on our behalf.

At the start of March, on a day off from the office I felt prompted to go to work anyway. On a notice board was a message asking me to urgently contact a lady — a friend of Patricia Cook who was involved in the flat search for us. The voice at the other end of the phone explained excitedly

"There's a flat just become available but you'll have to move fast, Roy. If you don't go this evening, it'll be gone."

So we set out with Patricia in tow to look at the flat, driving to an area of Lausanne we'd never been to before. The rather nervous landlord showed us around. It was perfect and immediately felt like home. But this was Switzerland. What hoops would we need to go through to get it?

"What paperwork do we need, sir?" I asked in my best French.

"Aucun, monsieur," he said. "Je n'ai besoin de rien."

Had I understood him correctly? No paperwork, no references, no deposit? He didn't need anything? I looked to Patricia for confirmation but the landlord smiled, put his hand in his pocket, gave us a bunch of keys and asked, "When would you like to move in?"

I wanted to stammer out, "But you don't know anything about us. And you don't know YWAM, so you've no reason to trust us." Instead I held my breath as he added, "Since March has already begun you don't need to pay rent until April 1st". This was no April Fool, God was continuing to direct our paths; He was making sure we felt loved and welcomed in our new country.

It had been dark when we arrived at the flat so we had no idea what lay outside. A rat-infested alleyway? No, not possible in Switzerland. A brick wall, metres away from our windows? Some snag that darkness had hidden?

When we went back in daylight some days later to start moving in, we gasped in amazement. Stretched out before us was Lake Geneva with the snow-capped French Alps beyond. God gives in abundance, more than we could ever ask or think. He is never mean with his children. We were glad to trust such a Father and so very thankful.

Now we had to attend to the girls' school needs. Another linguistic and bureaucratic hurdle for both them and us, we thought. But Amy excelled and slotted right into a French-speaking school for children with special needs without so much as a whimper. As Shirley set out the breakfast things one morning, Amy plonked herself down at the table, with a "Merci, maman." Our little Down's Syndrome daughter would be bilingual!

Soon Amy fell sick and we had to keep her off school for a few days. God will deal with this, we thought. So we prayed that she would get better. Nothing happened. More prayer. More sickness. Why wasn't God meeting our needs? We'd got used to Him doing that and we anticipated Him providing a fast answer. Now we'd have to take her to the doctor which would mean a huge bill. Even the basic appointment cost a fortune — never mind any treatment he might prescribe.

At this stage we were insured with an international company whose excess was one hundred US Dollars for each medical bill. *"How many of these might lie ahead?"* I asked myself. But worry took a back seat as I began to sense a new way that God was going to deal with us. It was another stage of trust. This time, instead of instantaneous healing, I watched as He provided the finance for us to pay every health bill that came our way. Gradually we were getting to know God's ways and how diverse they were.

In those early days Amy was seen by a Swiss cardiologist who was on the verge of retiring. While examining the on-screen image of her heart, he called for his colleagues to come and have a look. "Who performed this surgery?" he exclaimed. "In all of my long career I've never seen such a good repair. Please give me the name of the surgeon and the hospital address, I want to write and congratulate him!"

After our first Easter in Switzerland, Catherine was able to start at a Christian school that had originally been founded by YWAM. But how would things work out for her? We had focused so much on Amy and were aware that we needed to shower extra love on Catherine. Were we asking too much of her to move her from the security of home and an English-speaking environment? Didn't she need an extra measure of protection after all that we had gone through as a family? But we needn't have worried. When she came home on the first day she chatted about the little boy who'd been seated at the desk next to hers. "He's Arnoud — English Mum and Swiss Dad. And he speaks French and English. He helped me all day." Within six months she was speaking French like a native, Swiss accent and all.

Everything seemed to be falling into place: for our girls in their schools, for me working with Loren and now with our very nice, reasonably priced flat with an amazing view to call home. But someone was left out. What was Shirley to do and be?

Expanding Horizons

"Make the coffee and sandwiches and lead the women's group. Keep house, feed the man in your life and nurture your children." Was that to be Shirley's role? I knew my gifted and strong wife wouldn't settle for anything less than what God had in mind. Thankfully YWAM doesn't limit the talented women in its ranks. But how was God going to use Shirley and her gifts? She's a people person, clear thinking and able to organise. Where would she feel fulfilled? It didn't take long for someone to see her potential and ask her to oversee the operational side of things in YWAM Lausanne, setting up systems to help things function more smoothly. This meant lots of interaction with other staff, so Shirley began to make friends as well as use her talents.

In the meantime, I was battling with the complexities of scheduling Loren Cunningham's travels. You'd think with the whole of South West Trains having been at my fingertips, it would have been a piece of cake — but not so. Now I was dealing with an individual rather than a line of carriages and it was very different. I had to handle a torrent of emails and juggle speaking schedules, hospitality arrangements, connections with planes, trains (yes, they were OK!), boats and buses, as well as the inevitable piles of books that had to arrive at Amsterdam or Buenos Aires or Canberra in the requisite numbers. On top of this, I oversaw the office accounts.

In the middle of our busyness we needed a comfortable place to retreat to. So our flat — furnished as it was with second hand beds, a third hand sofa and a fourth hand wobbly table, really mattered. That wobbly table became the symbol of all that frustrated us as it tipped over continually, spilling mugs of tea or plates of biscuits with relentless regularity. And, mopping up cloth in hand yet again, a determined Shirley muttered, "It's got to go. Money or no money, we need a new table. I've spent as much time on my knees cleaning up as I do praying." I was wise enough not to contradict this clear exaggeration and hastily planned a shopping trip the next day. We both knew we didn't have the money to buy a new table, unless we dipped into the savings left over from my Railway days and we had strongly felt that it wasn't time to touch those yet.

Regardless, the next morning we went to a good furniture shop, ordered a sturdy table and waited for God to act. I was thankful that we didn't have to put down a deposit. But the waiting time between ordering and delivery was going to be interesting. Practice makes perfect — and I was certainly getting a lot of "waiting for God" practice.

When a letter arrived from the tax authorities in Britain the following day, I did wonder if God was going to stretch this faith test with a large tax demand. Instead the letter contained a refund cheque. I did my rapid British pounds to Swiss francs calculation, and discovered that yet another small miracle had occurred — the cheque was for exactly the same amount as the table we'd just ordered. God had timed it to the moment when Shirley could tolerate the table no longer. He will not test us beyond what we can bear — even when the test is as small as a frustratingly wobbly table. Daily, our Swiss table, which has now moved with us around several countries, is an ongoing reminder of God's wonderful provision.

Furniture requirements met, we wondered what need our loving heavenly Father would turn to next. This business of trusting was beginning to feel exciting, not scary. So we were not surprised when our first visitors from Farnham, John and Glenys Wilkinson, made the perfect suggestion. Their son owned a second home in southern France — why didn't we take the opportunity of a summer holiday there? They didn't know just how much we needed a break after the exhaustion of a major house move, learning new jobs and adapting to a foreign culture. But God had our holiday planned before we'd even given it a thought. Heading across the border in our well-packed car and driving for seven hours through France was such a novelty for former island dwellers like us! We were used to queuing to board ferries and flights, schedules and pre-planning. God had even made the holiday journey easy.

A few weeks after our time away, Shirley set off for the biannual University of the Nations (UofN) workshop in Seoul, South Korea. After all she'd had to handle over the years since Amy's birth, it was good to see her fly off to new adventures and begin to experience YWAM's international vision. The UofN is YWAM's training arm operating in 160 countries, teaching 600 courses and seminars in nearly 100 languages. So while I held the fort back in Lausanne, Shirley began to dream bigger dreams, getting a taste of Loren and Darlene's global mission and networking with lots of like-minded people. When I met her in the airport concourse, she could scarcely wait to tell me, "Roy, it was wonderful. I think I know what God wants me to do in YWAM. I went to a seminar about Family Ministries and I felt such a tug at my heart. I believe that's where I belong."

It wasn't long before I also flew out of Geneva Airport. As Loren's Scheduling Assistant, we decided that I should go with him to Central America on one of his outreach journeys to experience the other side of my planning for him. I watched Loren work with awe. In each of the seven countries we visited he was full of fervour and eagerness, preaching and sharing with anyone who would listen. Jet lag didn't slow him down, exhaustion didn't stop him and separation from family wasn't even an issue. I was truly glad to have such a mentor and friend. But for me it was a challenge being away from my family, especially when I received an email telling me that I wasn't to worry, but Amy was in hospital.

Another child at school had scratched her arm causing it to bleed and the wound quickly became infected. From this small incident, she developed septicaemia which was life-threatening because of her heart condition.

Once again God was ordering events since, on the very same day, Richard and Karen Stubberfield arrived in Switzerland to see Shirley and the girls. They were able to take care of Catherine while Shirley was at the hospital with Amy. Before our friends returned to Farnham, Amy had more or less recovered. Throughout Amy's life we've encountered God's special envoys, responsive people who listen to Him and react quickly and eagerly, who don't mind their plans being disrupted and who delight to serve. I don't know what kind of break the Stubberfields had in Lausanne — I'm sure it was different from what they'd imagined — but once again the Divine Scheduler was putting things in place for us. Our longstanding friend Morag lived around the corner, as did Patricia Cook. Both of them helped us out on many occasions. When Catherine decided as a teenager, that she'd like to have a godmother, she chose Patricia who has faithfully prayed for her over many years.

Later during the Central American trip, we had an amusing encounter while in transit through El Salvador Airport. Loren was keeping himself to himself, reading in a corner to pass the time when I spied a group of teenagers wearing "King's Kids" t-shirts. Approaching them, I asked what King's Kids was — even though I already knew the answer. They explained that it's a youth and children's ministry which is a part of Youth With A Mission and they were returning to North America from outreach in Brazil. "What is that mission and who founded it?" I asked. When they told me about Loren, I played the trump card: "Would you like to meet him? He's sitting just over there." The young peoples' reactions were priceless. Loren was happy to chat with them and sign their outreach diaries. I've no doubt that the encounter made a lasting impact on them.

During our second Spring in Switzerland, Shirley took a full time course at YWAM Lausanne's School of Biblical Studies (SBS). This was a twelve-week, intensive training that involved reading the entire Bible and learning how to analyse the different genres thoroughly. She also studied how to teach, preach and lead a small-group bible study. There was a lot of homework, but in spite of the demands of study and being a mother, she came away at the end of the course with a very high grade. Shirley was beginning to get equipped for the ministry which would follow. We didn't know how that was all going to work out but we knew that God was leading gently, step by step.

The end of the SBS coincided with the start of the school summer holidays and we felt we should plan a family outreach based around Shirley's recent training. That summer, YWAM Latvia was to celebrate its fifth anniversary; Loren and Darlene were invited to the celebrations. Only a few years previously, Latvia had shaken off the shackles of the Soviet communist empire and we were keen to minister there. We thought it would make the perfect fit and made contact with a missionary couple that we knew from Northern Ireland now working in Riga, the Latvian capital. They said they'd be happy for us to partner with them in their Baltic nation. This meant we could all be a part of the YWAM Latvia celebrations as well.

There was just one snag in our plan for the summer. The couple we were to stay with in Riga were hosting other people and wouldn't have room for us until their other guests had left. Unexpectedly we found ourselves with ten days free at the beginning of our two-month trip.

An exciting solution for how to fill the time presented itself. Although we'd never visited nor knew anyone who worked there, the YWAM centre at Restenäs, on the west coast of Sweden, had been of interest to me for nearly five years. It was the alternative place I had started to consider when our first trip to Lausanne didn't have the intended result that we had thought it would. YWAM Restenäs had been going through significant financial challenges and I'd been phoned a couple of times by a staff member asking if Loren could visit to help them. Through booking his tickets and being in contact with Restenäs, I knew that I would like to go someday too.

We became aware of an inTouch Gathering which was to take place there during the first week of our girls' school break. These gatherings are part of the YWAM Associates ministry which is aimed at past and present YWAMers, their supporters, friends and pastors etc. We felt this would give us a good experience of YWAM in a different country and the timing was perfect. We decided to register.

In those days, flights were not as cheap as now, so I had fun planning another route — a train trip up through Germany and into Denmark where our carriage was loaded onto a ferry taking it across the Øresund to Sweden. A different boat from Stockholm took us to Finland; more trains to Helsinki, yet another boat — this time to Estonia — and finally a bus from Tallinn to Riga. Shirley sighed as she contemplated this "interesting" route with two young children and a pile of suitcases.

But when we got to Restenäs, we knew that every last, exhausting moment of the journey had been worthwhile. We felt at home there, like we were meant to be part of the place — and the inTouch Gathering was exceptional. However, the financial challenges for YWAM there hadn't gone away by the time we arrived. There was a real danger that if the YWAMers in Restenäs couldn't pay the mortgage instalment due at the end of our week at inTouch, they might lose the property. The work there could come to an end, so it was decided to take an offering.

Shirley and I wanted to donate and prayed about how much to give. I knew that we had next to nothing in our bank account. Nevertheless, I felt that we were to give two hundred pounds in faith. I was more than a little shocked when Shirley announced after praying that the amount she felt we were to give was more like eight hundred! We'd heard Loren teach (somewhat tongue in cheek) in Lausanne that if a couple prays and gets different figures for giving to an offering, they should then add the two amounts together.

My thought was that since we didn't have two hundred pounds any more than we had a thousand, writing a cheque for the larger amount made little difference. God was going to have to honour our obedience, and for Him, finding the extra eight hundred pounds wasn't going to be any problem at all. We had our British cheque book with us and wrote the cheque knowing that we'd have a couple of weeks' grace before it would be cashed in. We'd never done anything like this before and were intrigued as to what the outcome would be. But we didn't doubt that we had done the right thing.

Once the Gathering was over, and with a couple of days to fill, we went on to Lapland. Crossing the Arctic Circle on a comfortable Finnish train, we brought the girls to visit Santa Claus — in July. We've a feeling that perhaps the 'Santa' we met was a Christian. He showed a lot of interest in why we lived in Switzerland, what we did in YWAM and also my work for Loren. He kept us talking for quite some time, even as the queue to see him built up behind us. It was a special day for our family, one where we built lasting memories.

Arriving in Riga two days later, we quickly jumped into the purpose of our trip. We went on prayer walks, helped at a children's camp and Shirley led some Bible studies. We also felt we should give a donation towards the ministry of the couple hosting us. It was nowhere near the £1,000 that went to Restenäs but we didn't know where these funds would come from either. We simply knew that we were meant to do it. The anniversary celebrations for YWAM Latvia were enjoyable and soon it was time for me to fly back to Switzerland for a week while Shirley and the girls remained in Riga. Loren hadn't minded my being away for the summer as long as I kept up with my work whilst gone. He'd asked me to return to Lausanne for a week in the middle of the outreach to check on things in the office.

A substantial pile of mail awaited me. As I worked my way through it, I came to a letter from the accountant of our sending church. There was no such thing as internet banking back then so we relied on periodic paper statements from our bank. The accountant apologised for not informing us beforehand of a number of gifts from supporters that he'd transferred into our personal account. There were two significant things about this transfer. Firstly, it came to a similar amount as the total of the two gifts we'd recently made to Restenäs and in Riga; secondly, it had been sitting in our account for at least five weeks. The funds were there before we had even left Lausanne for Sweden!

We learned another important lesson through this experience — God will always honour those who step out in obedience to Him. That honouring is unique to the individual and to their situation. All it requires is an obedient heart and open hands. We have experienced His creative provision for us many times over the years and He is always faithful.

Back in Latvia I found all going well. The rest of the outreach passed quickly and, before we knew it, the time came to make the long overland journey to Lausanne. We hopped on a bus to Vilnius, the capital of Lithuania and found it a charming place. We'd reserved a hotel room as we had an early start on the train to Warsaw and Berlin the following day. The hotel gave us an unexpected and welcome upgrade to a suite where we could relax and get a good night's sleep — one which was free from the fleas which had plagued us where we'd been housed in Riga. This made a big difference (especially to Shirley) as the entire journey over land took three days from start to finish. We sensed it was a special "thank you" from our heavenly Father for spending our summer holidays in His service.

We were only at home in Lausanne for one full day before the girls returned to another year at school. Driving to YWAM Lausanne a few days later, we were shocked to hear on the radio that a Swissair plane had crashed off the coast of Canada. It was believed that all on board had perished. One of those who died was a young man on his way to be a staff member on the Lausanne DTS that was due to start in September. It was a sad day for all of us and we struggled to understand our Father's plans in this. The young man's death also meant that a gap needed to be filled quickly in the DTS staff team and Shirley was asked to fill it. After praying it through, she accepted. Her SBS course was now to be put to good use, much earlier than she had anticipated. We were able to balance most of the childcare and work responsibilities between us and were grateful for two flexible daughters who made it possible.

Towards the end of the year, Loren asked me to travel to South Africa to help with the University of the Nations Advisory Board meetings being held there. The Advisory Board is an international group consisting mainly of people in the business world who give input into YWAM's university. It was a stimulating time where I learned a lot from listening to wise and godly men.

We rounded up 1998 by going to Amsterdam with the DTS that Shirley was working with for a three-week Christmas and New Year outreach. Shirley enjoyed witnessing on the streets of the city, connecting readily with complete strangers. I was happier doing the practical arrangements. As I considered the year, I calculated that I'd been in thirty countries — even more than Loren himself. And I found I was developing an appetite for travel. So I was more than happy to travel by train to Hungary in February 1999 to help debrief the smaller team from the DTS which by then had travelled to Serbia. They were evacuated to Budapest after finding themselves in the middle of a political and military crisis as tensions between Serbia and NATO increased. Life in YWAM was certainly nothing like sitting behind a desk in the office at Waterloo!

Safely home and the DTS over, we anticipated that there would be a greater sense of routine in our lives and for a few months this was the case. Nevertheless, ever present on the horizon was Amy's health situation. She had a problem with one of her ears and needed to have surgery. We were still using the international health insurance company that we had been with since moving to Switzerland and, on applying to them to meet the costs of this, they informed us that this was the last ear operation they would pay for.

The surgery went ahead, but how were we to finance Amy's future health needs? Swiss insurance companies were beyond our reach and, though subsidies were available for low income families, the authorities had refused to give them to YWAMers, stating: "You chose to be poor, why should we help out?" On the other hand, we couldn't risk being uninsured for any further issues regarding Amy's hearing. We felt prompted to go ahead and sign up with a Swiss company.

We were advised that once accepted by a Swiss company, we could apply for the state subsidy. We felt God had called us to serve in Switzerland and that we should honour the authorities there, so we were completely upfront about being YWAM staff. Somehow within weeks, and against all odds, we were granted the subsidy for the Swiss health insurance (which was more comprehensive than the international one we'd previously used).

Two things transpired following this episode. Firstly, not long after we were accepted for our subsidy, the local government tightened the conditions for applicants requesting them in future. Almost immediately after that, our previous international insurers were told by the Swiss authorities that they could no longer operate in Switzerland. They'd done nothing wrong, it was simply for technical reasons. Anyone insured by them had to leave that company and transfer to a Swiss scheme. Had we not switched to our Swiss scheme exactly when we did, it would have been far less likely that we could have benefited from state assistance in the way that it happened. Not for the first nor the last time, God had directed our paths down to the last details of timing.

Shortly after Amy's ear operation, we were visiting a YWAM centre in Italy, a few hours' drive from Lausanne. We noticed a brochure promoting a three-month long Leadership Training School at YWAM Norway's main training centre in Grimerud, near the Winter Olympic city of Hamar. The brochure captivated us; the subjects to be covered looked intriguing and would be helpful to our ministry. We just knew that we were to apply.

The school was to start a few days into the year 2000 and would have a strong focus on Europe. We were increasingly realising that we were called to all of Europe, not just Switzerland. God had given us a strategic location at the heart of the continent we love. Where would He take us next on our European journeyings? We sensed with excitement that there was much more to come.

A Stake in the Ground

" Blow here, sir," said the policeman, in impeccable English. Shirley eyed me with concern as I blew into the breathalyser, lest something might register an unacceptable level of alcohol. Unlikely as it was, we didn't want to be declared persona non grata in Norway. This was my first — and so far only — breathalyser; it happened on a Sunday morning very early in the new millennium at the port in Oslo. I didn't reckon to be looking particularly suspicious and had been driving in a straight line (albeit only down the ferry ramp and onto the dockside), but it was a new experience.

We were making one of our very long journeys but, to Shirley's great relief, I'd abandoned the railway timetable and not a single train or bus was involved. Now we were en route to the Leadership Training School (LTS) in Norway. We'd left Switzerland two days earlier, and a comfortable nineteen-hour boat ride from Germany's Baltic Coast brought us to Scandinavia where we'd be studying for the next three months. We couldn't have known it at the start of our Nordic adventure, but it was to be another of those life-changing experiences.

Having been declared fit to continue, we spent the last couple of hours of our long northbound journey driving to YWAM Grimerud where a comfortable but compact living space had been prepared for the four of us.

Our class was made up of over fifty students. Around half of us were from outside Norway, the remainder being nationals. Thankfully, the LTS was completely in English. Early in the course we all wrote our personal mission statements. This consisted of twenty values with appropriate Bible verses linked to them. It was a helpful way to start our studies.

A major portion of the LTS, making up fifty percent of the grades, was working on a new visionary project for missions. The proposal had to be detailed — backed up with facts as well as a step by step timeline. We were training to be leaders in YWAM and needed to know how to transform vision into reality. Shirley and I both developed projects to do with families who work in missions; what we learned through that process has been useful ever since. Other subjects on the course included: God's heart for Europe, Personality Types (using the DISC Test which I found extremely helpful), Work/Rest balance, The Character of a Leader and Financial Management.

As is usual in most YWAM training schools, a week of lectures was given over to each specific subject. Every week a different speaker lectured on his or her subject of expertise.

One particular morning's teaching in the Financial Management week had an unexpected impact that completely changed the direction of our lives.

The speaker, Earl Pitts from Canada, was explaining that in the Old Testament those who were considered to be wealthy didn't necessarily have large amounts of money. Instead, they may have owned a lot of land, animals or even properties. These things were to be left as inheritances for the next generation. Earl encouraged each of us to think about what we were planning to leave for our descendants.

This wasn't something I'd ever considered. Living day to day on the generosity of supporters didn't give us much opportunity to save for the future. We were paying monthly rent on our flat in Lausanne, but that wasn't helping us to put anything aside for our own tomorrows, let alone those of Catherine and Amy.

Five years had passed since my boss on the Railway had offered me the redundancy package which had allowed us to keep our savings in the bank. It was now clear what that money was to be used for: we'd be tenants no more but were to buy our own home in Switzerland. It would be our stake in the ground, something to show that we identified with the country of our calling as well as being an inheritance for our daughters. God had not only spoken about our present, but also our girls' futures.

Before we could even think seriously about buying a place anywhere, we had to finish our course in Norway. We enjoyed those weeks, profiting enormously from all that we learned. An unexpected bonus came with Amy's social development. Her school teachers in Lausanne had expressed concern that we were taking her away from formal education for three months. To a degree they were correct to be worried. However, the relational input she received far outweighed what she missed at school back in Switzerland. In Norway she learned a small measure of independence from her parents and made new friends. She felt more comfortable than ever before when she wandered around on her own, chatting with everyone she met on the way.

We studied with wonderful fellow students and made friends for life. Occasionally we still work alongside some of them. From Lapland in the Arctic Circle to Italy and Romania in the south of Europe, we've been involved in different ministries that are a direct result of connections made during that exceptional course.

On returning to Lausanne at the beginning of April, we set about looking for the ideal home. It took some time and there were false starts along the way. We initially hoped to live somewhere close to YWAM Châtel, halfway between Lausanne and Geneva. This was now the YWAM centre we associated with most since Loren Cunningham's recent return to Hawai'i.

I had stopped working for Loren soon after he left Switzerland. Now that we lived half a world apart, it had become a challenge to keep up with all that needed to be done for him. I'll always be grateful for his patience and encouragement, as well as the privilege of learning so much from such a humble, godly man.

In the meantime, I'd taken up new administrative responsibilities with YWAM Family Ministries in Switzerland. Still searching for a place to buy and wanting to have the deposit available, we transferred our savings from Britain to our bank in Lausanne. On the same day we made the transaction, the British pound was at its strongest against the Swiss franc during our entire fourteen years of living there! With the good exchange rate in our favour, a significant difference was made to the amount we now had available to purchase our Swiss property — once we'd found it. We weren't to know at the time that the pound would never be that strong again; however, we were conscious of God's blessing and provision when we realised just how many francs our life savings were able to buy.

Keeping busy with ministry activity in Châtel, I set up several seminars there. We also decided to run the first Swiss inTouch Gathering in the summer of 2002. It was modelled on the one we'd attended four years earlier in Restenäs, Sweden. Some forty people came to Châtel from many countries around the world. We had thought it would be a one off. How wrong we were.

Eventually we found somewhere to live in the small village of Montcherand, a twenty-minute drive from Lausanne. It was a lovely property that had formerly been the village forge. Situated in a peaceful location with amazing views of God's creation, the building was more recently part of a Christian school that had closed. Now it had been converted into several flats. The owners gave us a generous deal since we not only bought an apartment to live in but an adjoining studio-flat right next door.

It was a miracle that we were able to obtain a mortgage in Switzerland, a country renowned for its conservative banking system. A *real* miracle given that we were offered a very cheap fixed-rate mortgage lasting for five years. "That's the best deal I've ever come across" the Christian estate agent who accompanied me to the bank remarked as the interview concluded. "I've never seen an interest rate that low."

With grateful hearts we moved once again, just in time for Catherine and Amy to begin the academic year, taking their school buses from right outside our home.

Montcherand isn't especially close to any of the YWAM centres in French-speaking Switzerland. However, five of them — including Châtel — are an easy drive away. I worked from an office in our studio which was also used for hospitality, meetings and counselling appointments with local people. We drove to YWAM whenever we needed to meet with our co-workers; a monthly highlight was morning worship at the YWAM House of Prayer near Yverdon.

Shirley joined a women's Bible Study group and her French language skills quickly improved. Through her contacts in that group we joined a church in Vallorbe. As time passed, we became more involved there. Shirley served on the leadership team for three years; she ran Bible studies and counselling groups while we both worked with the young people. They were fulfilling years which kept us busy. At one stage Shirley was wearing nine 'hats' between her commitments to YWAM and our church. We were YWAMers living in the local community and we loved it.

Occasionally I'd be given an opportunity to do some temporary work in the mailroom of a company not far from Montcherand. Often the offers came in just when we needed the extra money. I once did a project for the company which involved having to learn the Excel computer program. It was very timely because I was aware that knowing it would help in my YWAM work. I had been struggling to get to grips with it on my own — now I was getting paid to learn it.

One day the company called me out of the blue asking me to come in the next weekend to work on an extra project. It just happened to coincide with three days we'd already committed to help another missionary organisation run their staff conference. Even though the extra income would have helped, there was no way I could say "yes" to the company. The conference – where we encountered a diverse group of missionaries with experiences very different from our own — went well. At the final meeting our new acquaintances approached us with an envelope. They had taken an offering for those of us who had worked to make their event so successful. Our share of that collection was the exact equivalent of what I would have earned had I spent the weekend working at the company. The added bonus was the satisfaction of meeting and serving fellow missionaries. We couldn't put a price on that.

Our God is consistent in the creativity of His provision for us; rarely do we know what is coming next. We had a small patch of land on our property which hadn't been tended for years. It was a tangled mess of rocks, litter, weeds and brambles, so I set about restoring it. This gave both fulfillment and a sore back! In our first spring I sowed potatoes — something I'd not done before — anticipating a harvest in the autumn. Watching our plants and vegetables grow as the summer progressed gave much satisfaction.

By early August we had received no income for a while. We were working on our fourth inTouch Gathering where our meals were all supplied. A looming concern niggled me — how would we manage once the camp was over?

When we got home I delayed walking into the kitchen. I knew I would find sparse cupboards, a nearly empty freezer and no fresh food whatsoever. Somehow we had to make these meagre provisions stretch out until our next support cheque came.

We started to unpack the car when I noticed Shirley gazing at our vegetable patch. "Roy, the potato flowers are starting to droop over. Why don't you dig one up to see if it's edible?" I had thought they wouldn't be ready yet, but still followed her advice; it looked fine so I carried on. When there were no more left in the ground we weighed them. On that summer evening we harvested seventeen kilos of tasty potatoes.

We all enjoy potatoes and were thankful for this timely provision. We got by with them, plus the small quantity of food we already had in our home, until the next sum of money arrived. We had a tangible sense that, as we trusted the Lord, we *could* dwell in the land of our calling and enjoy safe pasture (Psalm 37:3). We identified so completely with verse twenty-five: "*In all my years I have never seen the* LORD *forsake a man who loves him; nor have I seen the children of the godly go hungry*" (TLB).

We lived for seven happy years in Montcherand. As Amy grew older and approached adulthood, we knew that change was on the horizon — especially since she couldn't stay in school for much longer. Life would not remain the same. Even so, I had absolutely no inkling of what God had prepared for us next.

The Land of our Fathers

"It's time for us to move to Ireland," Shirley announced as she walked through our front door after returning from a visit to her parents. Taken by surprise and not seeing how it could be a good location for us, my instant reaction was to resist. Given that most of our work was in Switzerland or neighbouring countries, I couldn't work out her logic.

We'd spent a couple of weeks in Northern Ireland during the previous autumn when it was cold and damp for much of the time. Looking at clumps of moss on the pavements when out to buy the paper one morning, I said to myself, *"I'm so glad that we don't live here."*

Once I'd had time to understand the reasons behind Shirley's suggestion, I agreed to seek God for a clear word about moving (while secretly hoping that none would come). Shortly afterwards, I went to work on a YWAM event in Jerusalem. With a flight of several hours ahead of me, I thought I'd re-read the book where I had found the original verse which God had used to speak to us about going into YWAM. I couldn't remember the title but knew it was written by a New Zealander.

I picked up what I thought was the right book, put it in my carry-on bag and went to the airport. Once in the air, I started to read it but quickly realised that it wasn't the one I thought. Since it was a YWAM story and I had nowhere else to go, I kept reading anyway.

Somewhere over Austria, I came to a chapter about guidance. A verse leapt off the page at me: *"Go back to the land of your fathers and to your relatives and I will be with you"* (Genesis 31:3). As soon as I'd read it, I knew it was God's guidance. It made sense even though Wales is the land of *my* fathers — it's Ireland where Shirley's fathers come from.

I sent Shirley a quick message after landing to tell her about the verse, got to work and quickly put thoughts about Ireland to the back of my mind. They surfaced again once I was home in Montcherand but I started to backtrack. I knew that the verse was God's way of speaking to me, but was still very happy living where we were. I wanted to stay put, not to have to face the reality of leaving behind a life I was so content with.

Just after all of this, we'd started to take a serious look at Amy's future care. She was well into her teenage years and we were concerned about what her adult life would hold. Within a couple of years, she would finish school in Yverdon to enter a whole new way of life. We needed to weigh up the options.

They were quickly narrowed down to just one suitable possibility in our local area. Before getting the opportunity to visit, we 'happened' to meet the mother of a friend at a social event. This lady had a daughter who'd recently been resident at the same place we were considering for Amy. Her face grew serious as we mentioned the thoughts of our own daughter going there; she gave reasons why the place would not be appropriate for her.

We were back to square one and it didn't take long to come to the conclusion that Amy wouldn't have a very fulfilling future if we stayed where we were. The verse I'd received on the way to Israel was now increasing in relevance. But it was still challenging to think of moving to Northern Ireland.

Part of the issue back then was that YWAM's only location in the Province was in Belfast — a city which, at the time, I had no desire to be anywhere near. Fortunately, God is patient. I believe the timing of what I'd read on the plane was to give me several months in which to process the enormity of a move.

With slightly heavy hearts at the thought of living in Belfast, we made contact with YWAM Ireland. Heavy hearts or not, our desire was to obey God. I knew that I could trust Him to be with us if we were to make the move. He had promised to do so.

We had a good conversation with the leader of YWAM Belfast. To our astonishment, he told us that YWAM Ireland was being given a large building in Rostrevor. Located on the shores of Carlingford Lough and well away from Belfast, this property had been owned by another Christian ministry for many years. Most of their staff were about to retire; they wanted to pass their building onto a different mission with younger personnel. They were giving it to YWAM which suddenly made the idea of moving to Northern Ireland more attractive.

We set to work arranging an international move that, until a few months previously, we had never imagined could happen. We subsequently discovered that I do have ancestors from my father's side who once lived in the same county as Rostrevor. In one sense, I, too, was returning to the land of some of my own fathers — as well as those of Shirley.

One of the things needing to be done in preparation for our new life in the Emerald Isle was to change our car for a right-hand drive vehicle. Five years previously, through miraculous provision, we'd been able to purchase a comfortable car that was well suited to all of the ministry trips we made. The car had maintained its value and we hoped to use the funds generated from selling it to get a good quality replacement.

In the run-up to the move, we were at the first inTouch in Germany. It was held at Hurlach Castle, the second property YWAM had ever purchased — just in time for the 1972 Munich Olympics. We met a young YWAM family on staff there who were expecting their third child and desperately needed a larger vehicle. "How much will you sell your car for?" the husband asked. His face dropped as he listened to our hoped-for price.

As we drove away from Hurlach at the end of the week, Shirley and I talked about offering our car to the family for a reduced price. We *knew* that we had to do something to help. Once back in Montcherand we prayed and felt we were to ask if they could afford around half its value. We emailed our offer which was quickly accepted. At peace with our decision, it still left us with a projected shortfall in being able to purchase a car for life in Northern Ireland. We were assured that God would open the right doors for this to happen — after all He had done it before.

He was already at work. Only a few days later, I received what I originally thought was an ominous email. It came from a man working at the charity which processes gifts made towards our financial support. "I'm sorry to have to inform you . . ." it began. My heart sank a little as I pondered the possibility of our support decreasing. The message continued, "we've made some miscalculations during the past few years." I imagined that the miscalculations referred to were overpayments. Would we be asked to repay a substantial amount?

Not so! The email concluded by informing us that it was we who were owed money and asking if we'd like it to be transferred to our account soon. The funds amounted to hundreds of pounds and enabled us to afford the right car for our needs after all.

The lesson gleaned from this experience was that whether we'd offered our Swiss car at a lower price or not, the extra funds were going to come our way anyhow. If we hadn't obeyed what we felt was God's voice in making the offer to our German co-workers, we would have been richer financially — but would have lost out on the priceless opportunity to be used in blessing others.

At around the same time, Catherine was finishing her college education and wanted to go to a big year-end party organised by the students. "I'm not keen on it," I tried to say gently, explaining my reasons. It was an all-night event held at the lakeside in Yverdon where I was sure things would be happening that I didn't want her to see, and much less experience.

"But *everyone* will be there; they'll laugh at me if I'm not. I really do want to go."

Other fathers will identify with my dilemma. Catherine was not of age and still under my parental authority; I was desperate to protect her. She repeated that she wanted to be part of the celebration. I wondered if this was my moment to let go, to release her to find her own path in life? Shirley was away so I couldn't process the situation with her. In the end, I reluctantly gave permission.

A couple of hours before the start of the party, a torrential thunderstorm broke out with no sign of abating. The youngsters started to text each other that their event was postponed for three nights. Catherine seemed relieved but, feeling that this was only delaying my agony, I continued to pray.

On the day before the now-rescheduled party, Catherine approached me. "You know, Dad, I don't really want to go, but my friends all want me there. How can I get out of it?" I suggested that if I banned her from going, she'd have the perfect excuse. She readily agreed to the plan and I gave thanks!

That autumn we moved to Northern Ireland after fourteen happy years in Switzerland. It was a busy time. Along with four other YWAMers, we were excited to be part of pioneering in Rostrevor. Leaving Montcherand behind, we didn't feel the need to grieve as we expected to return at least a couple of times each year in connection with YWAM and also for holidays.

Our initial intention had been to sell our Swiss studio. We wanted to use the proceeds to pay off the mortgage on our main flat next door. The plan was then for the flat to double up as an ongoing investment as well as being a bolt-hole for ourselves and other friends to use when needed. We sold the studio to a missionary who had worked in Belgium for many years and was returning to retire in Switzerland. He wanted to live near his son and grand-children who happened to be our next-door neighbours in Montcherand.

Back in the newly acquired YWAM Rostrevor building, we'd been allocated a flat that hadn't been lived in for a few years. It needed a lot of work to make it habitable. Amy's room had moss growing on the carpet and, when we lifted it up, we found a nest of unpleasant insects. On the bright side, once that carpet was replaced and Amy had settled into her refurbished room, we realised that the damp Irish climate was better for her lungs than the drier air in Switzerland.

Catherine had come with us and, once we'd started to get established, began to think about her next step. She decided to go to Kona to do her own Discipleship Training School but first had to get a visa. We made an appointment for her compulsory interview with the American Embassy in London.

Time was short, Christmas was approaching and the weather was closing in over the British Isles — with Ireland about to be hit by the worst winter in fifty years. All flights were cancelled so Catherine and I went by boat across to Wales where we took our chances on a train to London. The rail network was in a mess because of heavy snowfalls, but we prayed hard. God heard; we made it in good time for the appointment.

Having prayed so much about the transport situation, I didn't give much attention to interceding for the interview itself. After all, Catherine only wanted to be in the US for three months so I couldn't foresee a problem. I was more concerned about getting back to Northern Ireland in time for Christmas. Not permitted to attend the interview, I went to a nearby cafe. Looking up after the last sip of coffee, I was puzzled to see a clearly upset Catherine coming through the door. "My visa has been refused," she said through the tears. "I can't do the DTS."

"We don't have to accept this," I replied. "God spoke clearly to you and we're not giving up!"

Among the reasons given for the refusal was that Catherine had planned to travel on a Swiss passport. She now lived in the UK and had no means of supporting herself while on the DTS. We would not take "no" for an answer — she was supposed to go. We were going to try again. Appeals are not permitted against visa refusals so it meant re-applying from scratch.

Firstly we had to get back home. Through a series of just-in-time connections, we made it by train and boat as far as Dublin. We took a taxi from the port to the main bus station, only to find every departure cancelled because of the awful weather. No bus was going anywhere . . . apart from the one we needed to take us back to Northern Ireland. The driver went slowly through the snow and ice but at least we got there. We were relieved as a night in a cold bus station did not appeal.

Catherine managed to arrange a new appointment to be interviewed. This time, and with much prayer backing, the visa was granted. God was in it right from the beginning; it was as if her DTS started before she'd even left us because she was learning key lessons in perseverance.

She went early in the new year and once she was about a month into the course had to make her decision of where to go on the outreach phase of her DTS. The entire school was going to China, with eight locations in the country to choose from. The idea was that each student would seek God for an indication as to where they should serve. Catherine wanted input from her earthly dad as well as her heavenly one. She emailed me a list of the possible locations (most of which I'd never heard of) and asked if I too could pray for guidance. Hoping that she would hear directly from God for herself, I hesitated. I didn't want to influence the decision, but she seemed to really need my impressions too.

When praying, I wondered if Macau — a former Portuguese colony an hour's boat ride from Hong Kong — was the place for her. I felt the weight of the responsibility, what if I were to get it wrong? The next time we spoke she asked which place I'd 'received' for her when I prayed.

"I think it's Macau."

"That's what I got too!"

I reminded her that she was supposed to hear God's guidance for herself.

"I know; He gave me that impression too," came the reply. Catherine's faith was growing. She asked friends if they'd be willing to sponsor her and they gave generously. The outreach was based at a children's home founded by Marjory, a Brazilian YWAMer. As far as Catherine was concerned, it was a great success — so much so that she left

Macau promising to try and return with Shirley for their own mini-outreach later in the year.

Meanwhile, I had visited Montcherand to tie up some administrative affairs. This included an appointment at the tax office.

"You realise, now that you're non-resident, you will have to pay twenty percent of the value of your property in tax each year?" the clerk on the other side of the counter questioned — as if he expected me to have known.

This was a bombshell which was very hard to accept. It was clear we'd have to sell the flat that had meant so much to us.

It took a few months for a potential purchaser to express interest but eventually we had a buyer — a man working with Open Doors in Lausanne who wanted to invest in a buy-to-let property. The strong seller's market at the time meant we received an excellent offer.

Shortly after signing the deal, I felt God prompting me to transfer our Swiss funds as soon as possible to our British account. I went online and did it immediately. Overnight, new regulations were brought in by the Swiss Treasury which markedly affected the exchange rate to our disadvantage. By listening to God's prompting, we gained a significant amount just before the government intervention in the currency markets.

It helped us to leave Switzerland behind in the knowledge that our two properties had been sold to Christian buyers. Both the purchaser of the studio and the eventual tenants in the flat were in a time of transition when they moved to Montcherand; for us to watch events unfolding which included provision for other Christians was encouraging.

While this was happening, we became increasingly aware of how much we had underestimated the workload that we'd be doing in Rostrevor. It took its toll both on Shirley's health and on our commitments to YWAM internationally. Having received advice from concerned friends, we considered moving a short distance away from the YWAM centre. And now, thanks to the release of funds from Montcherand, we could afford to buy a place of our own in Northern Ireland.

The goal was to be close enough to remain involved with YWAM Rostrevor, but far enough away to be able to give more time to our broader responsibilities. One result of our move out would be to free up housing space in YWAM for new staff coming in. This was urgently needed as the ministry was growing rapidly.

I started the search for a home while Shirley was away with Catherine in Macau. True to her word, Catherine had taken her mum back to help out at the children's home she'd worked in during her DTS outreach.

"What's your budget?" the estate agent in Rostrevor asked, before suggesting we look at a house that wasn't in the area we'd initially been considering. As soon as we drove up, I knew it would be perfect for us. The challenge was to get hold of Shirley in Asia to see if she would feel the same way. We had not been able to communicate much while she was away.

During her devotional time the same morning (but six hours ahead of me), Shirley felt God ask, *"Would you trust Roy's judgement to make an offer on a good family home even if you couldn't see it for yourself?"* Just after my viewing, she was able to get on Skype to hear me enthuse about the house I'd just seen. She quickly agreed that I should make an offer.

Perhaps the most amazing aspect of this part of our story is that we were able to buy our new home without needing a mortgage. We were debt-free. What an incredible position to be in for unsalaried missionaries! This was due in part to the favourable exchange rates, both at the time of our original purchase in Switzerland — as well as when we sold years later. In the intervening years, the position of the pound dropped from strong to weak. On each occasion this worked in our favour. A seller's market in Switzerland had helped considerably because the value of our properties had increased substantially while we lived in them. A buyer's market in Northern Ireland, caused by recession, complimented the very real sense that we'd been in the right place at the right time for our home transactions.

Amy did very well from the start in Northern Ireland. She attended a vibrant school for those with learning difficulties and loved it. Learning only in English was a big plus so she quickly felt at home. When she was finally too old to go to school, she was given a place at a day centre run by "Prospects" — a Christian charity providing support to adults with special needs — where she received a warm welcome. "I'm too big for school," she would say with a huge grin, "I'm at Prospects now."

I Believe in Angels

"Roy, is that you?" a female voice asked hesitantly from a few feet away. It was January 2010, a few months before we moved to Northern Ireland. I was in transit through Washington DC, having just arrived from Kona. With a couple of hours to kill before my next flight to Switzerland, I was looking for a coffee shop when I heard the recognisable voice of Véronique who attended the same church as us in Vallorbe.

I'm not sure who was the most surprised. She'd just flown in from Geneva and was also connecting to another flight. It was mere coincidence that we passed each other at the same time in a very busy terminal. Or was it?

During the fortnight that I had been working in Kona, Véronique was preparing to leave Switzerland for a six-month voluntary stint at an orphanage in Mexico. Apprehensive about the approaching trip, she had called in to see Shirley who prayed specifically that God would provide an angel to help her along the way.

Shirley had no idea that her husband was to be the answer to that prayer! Véronique and I chatted over coffee before I took her to her gate and wished her "bon voyage". The timing of our chance meeting was incredible: both of our incoming flights were early which brought us to the terminal at the same moment. I didn't know that she'd be there on that day and wasn't looking for her. Talk about perfect timing — the master scheduler had been at work again.

The end of that year found us all in Kona once more, but this time we'd flown from Northern Ireland. One night towards the end of our work there, Shirley's phone rang in the small hours. The news wasn't good – her sister in Belfast was calling to tell us that their eighty-seven-year-old father had just passed away.

Eventually sleep came, although we woke up to another challenge. In many parts of Ireland, it's traditional for the deceased to be buried within two days. Shirley's Dad had requested this too. He died at lunchtime on a Friday; Ireland was ten time zones ahead of Hawai'i. If normal practice was to be adhered to, he would be laid to rest on Sunday. It's not possible to get all the way back from Hawai'i to Europe in less than two nights and, in a further complication, we were travelling on non-exchangeable tickets redeemed with air miles.

Pondering all of this, I went out to buy milk. It was unthinkable that we should miss my father-in-law's funeral but it seemed impossible to find a way of getting there in time. Shirley was sure there would be a solution but I couldn't think of anything remotely feasible. While I was at the shop, Shirley's sister rang her again. It seemed that the death certificate hadn't been issued before Friday evening in Ireland. The next possible time it could be done was after the weekend, on Monday. This meant the funeral would have to be delayed until Tuesday, the day that we were due to arrive back in Northern Ireland. When I returned with the milk, Shirley met me with the family's decision: since their Dad's wishes couldn't be fulfilled, they would postpone the funeral thus ensuring we could be there.

We never found out what prevented the death certificate from being issued on time; we were simply told that it was a technicality. This is one example of many divine interventions which stretch back over decades.

Working on the Railway had given me privileges of free travel, not just in Britain but in most European countries too. My first trip on a free international rail ticket was at age nineteen to a missions conference for European youth held in Lausanne. The "Continent" had been just somewhere on the other side of the Channel where people lived differently than the British. Until that experience I'd had no idea how accessible mainland Europe could be. This conference opened my eyes to the broadness of the Christian family; here I felt European for the first time. It was my maiden visit to Switzerland, the nation that since had such a major impact on the lives of everyone in our family.

After that eventful trip I went to Europe by train and boat whenever I had leave from my job. East Berlin and Budapest were among the cities I visited — at that time they were still behind the Iron Curtain. I met interesting people on and off trains, enjoying both planning and making the journeys. God was opening my eyes to the diversity of Europe and its peoples. Those backpacking trips when I was young, free and single were preparing me for a future missionary call to the whole of Europe.

I'm glad to have married someone who likes to experience new and diverse things. I met Shirley on an overland coach trip from London to Istanbul travelling through ten different countries. Along the way, I discovered that she had some Bibles to smuggle into one of them — communist Bulgaria. I'd encountered a woman of faith with an adventurous spirit and wanted to get to know her better.

Ever the romantic, I proposed to her at a Railway station north of Belfast several months later on Easter Sunday. Once we were married, Shirley, as a Railway wife, became entitled to free train travel too.

No matter what mode of travel we used, we've been aware of angels accompanying us. Sometimes it feels as if they work overtime to look after us. As YWAMers, we usually need to pay our own way for ministry trips so we've become experts at looking for good deals.

Once we'd been in Rostrevor for a while, I was asked to help administrate another inTouch in the United States. Having searched for the best ticket to get me there in good time, the most reasonable fare I came up with was from Dublin to Frankfurt with a connection from there to Los Angeles. One hundred and twenty pounds cheaper than going via London, the downside was a journey six hours longer. I wasn't terribly excited about spending so much time in the air, especially as the plane from Frankfurt would probably go right back over Ireland on its westward path. I booked the ticket regardless because the lower price justified the extra travel time.

Waiting in the departure lounge at five in the morning, we bleary-eyed passengers were disturbed to hear the bad news of a strike at Frankfurt Airport. The announcement advised of an indefinitely delayed departure. We were stuck with nowhere to go.

My transit through Frankfurt should only have lasted an hour. I knew that if I missed the connection to Los Angeles, I'd probably have to wait in Germany until the following day. Approaching the airline desk with a request to be rerouted via London, my plea was flatly refused. Lufthansa had given instructions that all passengers should still travel to Frankfurt to be rebooked there, and they weren't budging.

Resigned to my fate, I returned to my seat only to hear my name being paged a few minutes later. The airline had

had a change of heart. They would rebook me via London after all but I'd need to return to check-in to collect my luggage, receive new boarding passes and have my cases re-tagged. It seemed I was getting a free passage on the flights that would have cost so much extra had I originally paid to travel on them.

An airline agent directed me to make my own way back to check-in through the arrivals section. Once the sliding doors had closed behind me, I found myself in a completely sealed-off area with no apparent way out. It was so early in the morning that the hall through which I was supposed to exit was not yet open! I tried every door but with no success; they were all locked solid — including the one I'd just passed through one minute before.

Wondering how on earth I could get out of my airport prison, I spied a small door with a notice "Strictly Authorised Personnel Only". With no other choice, I 'authorised' myself to go through and ended up on the tarmac right beside the Lufthansa plane I should originally have been on. I made myself known to the baggage handlers who were searching for my case to offload, helpfully pointing it out to them. Being in an area forbidden to the public, they were taken aback to see me there.

They radioed for someone to collect me, suitcase and all. This time every door opened, getting me right back to the check-in area. The flight to London was fully booked in Economy Class, so now I was given an upgrade to Business — enjoying a nice hot breakfast on the way. The one hundred and twenty pounds that I'd saved seemed to be going even further.

My return ticket from America to Ireland a couple of weeks later was routed back through Heathrow. On boarding the short connecting flight, I could see that the person sitting in the seat next to mine was Willie Walsh, Chief Executive of British Airways. We were travelling on what turned out to not be a very good day for the airline. One delay compounded into another — although to be fair, most of them were not BA's fault. I kept my head down while the crew busily fussed over their Chief Executive.

Eventually the captain came on the loudspeaker to announce that our plane had a technical fault. We couldn't fly and would have to transfer to another plane. This took a while but, with the seat layout identical in the new one, at least we avoided more complications.

On the other side of the Irish Sea, Shirley and the girls were already on the seventy-five-mile drive to meet me in Dublin. It wasn't until they were inside the terminal that they knew my flight had a long delay. With no idea when I might take off, let alone get there, we messaged each other, wondering what to do. Eventually we decided that, as it was getting so late and Amy had school the following day, they should return without me. I would need to plan on making my own way home.

Asking if we'd met before — which we hadn't — Willie Walsh started to make conversation. After the pleasantries were over, I decided to take advantage of the situation.

Mentioning Shirley's one hundred and fifty mile wasted round trip, I asked if it was reasonable to expect compensation from the airline. Mr Walsh replied positively by asking for my business card. He wanted to text me his email address so that I could follow up my claim with him personally if it proved to be necessary. My card has the YWAM logo with our mission statement written in bold: "To Know God and to Make Him Known".

He was as good as his word, promptly texting his address and wishing me well when we finally disembarked several hours later. I sent my claim to the airline's customer relations department but heard nothing for a couple of months. I finally followed up by contacting Willie Walsh. Within days, the airline had offered me 10,000 air miles in compensation.

Later that year, Shirley, Amy and I flew to Gothenburg at the start of a three-week ministry trip. Driving once again to Dublin Airport — a place we now knew well — I left the other two with our cases at the terminal and continued to the long-term car parking. The paperwork for the car park, our preprinted boarding passes plus other necessary documents for the whole trip were in my carry-on bag, which stayed with me in the car.

Roadworks along the way slowed me down. The traffic was stop-start, stop-start and the clock was ticking. After finding a place to park, I waited at the bus shelter for the shuttle back to the terminal. The bus was late. I waited and waited, starting to get concerned. Retrieving the folder containing our boarding passes, I checked the deadline to be at the departure gate. When the crowded bus eventually came, I squeezed my way on, not realising that I'd left all the documents behind in the shelter.

Approaching the terminal, I became aware that the paperwork and I were not in the same place. Managing to get to the front of the bus, I talked to the driver who radioed his control office. The controller put out a message to the driver of the following bus who collected the papers which were still on the seat where I'd left them. He brought them to the terminal, where I was anxiously waiting.

We just made it to the check-in counter before it closed. Since we were en route to Sweden, I later posted about the incident on Facebook using some Abba song titles: "Mama Mia" at the realisation of my mistake, the "SOS" I'd sent out and how the bus drivers were "Super Troopers" for coming to the rescue. The post received a good bit of attention. One comedian suggested the words from another Abba song that I should have thought of: "I believe in Angels."

After our week in Sweden was over, we flew on to Romania for two more weeks of ministry. With no direct flights, we were routed via Munich. Our first plane was two hours late and the connecting flight was waiting. We hadn't been able to get advance seat allocations for it; by the time we breathlessly arrived at the gate, there were only middle seats left. Amy panicked at having to sit between strangers and didn't want to board. Wanting to avoid a delay, the airline upgraded her and Shirley to an empty Business Class section, enabling them to sit together in comfort.

Catherine believes in angels too. She made a further journey to Macau for a month but was apprehensive about making the long journey from Ireland alone. The boat trip from Hong Kong International Airport to her destination bothered her in particular. We prayed for angels to accompany her; God heard us again.

Sitting next to her on the flight to Hong Kong was a kindly resident of Macau. She offered to help Catherine with the boat transfer, guiding her through the passport channel in Macau that is usually reserved for nationals. This ensured a safe, speedy and straightforward arrival after her long solo journey.

There was another twist to this story. We strongly felt that we were only to give her ten pounds as emergency travel funds and no more. A test not only of her faith, but ours too; it wasn't at all easy to let her go with so little money. Sure enough, on the day she arrived, a large sum of money was deposited into her bank account by a generous supporter. This was sufficient to keep her going for the duration of her time in Macau.

All travellers have their tales of delays and frustrations — we are no exception. We're honoured to serve in different nations and are thankful for the myriad ways that our journeys have often been made smoother. We believe that the angels will be on standby as we continue to venture out where God calls us to go.

Jehovah Jireh,
Our Provider

ourteen years is a long time to resist an invitation but that's exactly what we'd been doing since the end of the Leadership Training School in Norway in the year 2000. We'd crossed into Sweden on the way home to Lausanne, called in at Restenäs and were invited for a meal with Kelvin, the director at the time. "I'll get to the point," he said as the dishes were being cleared away. "Will you come and join us here, we really need families like yours on our staff."

We promised to prayerfully consider the invitation as it was appealing in some ways. Restenäs would have been a wonderful place for our girls to grow up in — except that none of us could speak any Swedish. Would it have been fair on Amy to uproot her from so much that was familiar? She was six, so to expect a simple transition was unrealistic. The bottom line though was our connections in Lausanne and the ministries we were going back to. They had taken time to establish and we had no indication that it was time to pull away. Besides, we were going back to Switzerland to put our stake in the ground there, to purchase a property and become more rooted in the nation.

We knew we had to decline Kelvin's invitation, which he accepted with regret. Over the years, we would find ourselves back in Restenäs for different events — always loving the place, the people and the opportunities to serve there. Even though Kelvin eventually moved on, invitations to join the staff there still came from time to time. By the time we were well settled in Ireland, Tove from Denmark had taken over as director in Restenäs.

We'd known her since our early days in Lausanne when she and Shirley studied together on the School of Biblical Studies. She was also on staff at another Swiss YWAM centre for a few years. During frequent interactions at work and socially, the friendship grew.

As she developed her role as director in Restenäs, Tove became convinced that we should join her team, even to the extent of sending us a job description. We declined then — and on several subsequent occasions — citing Amy's challenges of not having any Swedish. As much as we enjoyed our visits to Sweden, we were rooted in Ireland. To contemplate another international move was not something we wanted to give a second thought to.

God had other plans! "I love Sweden; I want to live here," were the words which came out of Amy's mouth several times daily when we were working at the 2014 inTouch at Restenäs. Amy always felt at home there because we'd been so often, but this was a bolt out of the blue which we couldn't ignore. We needed to give the oft-repeated invitation some serious consideration.

Tove wasn't surprised to hear Amy say the same things to her. She seemed glad that we might finally be going to join her. We spent our last afternoon praying and processing together, each of us sharing desires and expectations while Amy listened intently. Shirley and I knew that, should we join YWAM Restenäs, it would be important for Amy to have her own role in its daily life. She's a people person who loves to help with easy-to-do practical tasks. To this end we expressed a desire to either live on the YWAM property or adjacent to it, thereby enabling Amy to come and go safely with a degree of independence.

Our full summer continued with several more camps in different parts of Europe. Shirley wasn't at all of them as she had separate family ministry events to attend in New Zealand, Singapore and West Africa. I'd worked in six different countries in the space of eight weeks so, when it was all over, I felt the need to have some introvert time. What better than to take a three-day drive from Ireland to Restenäs with the first shipment of our possessions?

At the exact moment I drove onto the YWAM Property, Tove sent me a text. "I've found your home," she enthused. A house directly adjacent to YWAM Restenäs had just come on to the market — something that rarely happens. The owners had wanted to sell the house several months previously (before we ever knew we'd be moving to Sweden), but were unable to. The "For Sale" signs eventually went up on the day I arrived there. I went to look at the outside, browsed the online sales brochure and decided to investigate further.

Marika, the tall, blonde Swedish estate agent advised me that, in order to make an offer on a property in Sweden, the buyer must prove they have the funds upfront. Once it has been established that a purchase is feasible, potential buyers are invited to bid. The price usually goes only one way — up!

Our assets were tied up in our Irish home so we didn't have the resources at hand to start bidding. We made contact with a Christian working in a Swedish bank. He got back the next day with a mortgage offer of up to eighty percent of the opening bid-price — and this without ever meeting us. We hoped we would never have to take out the mortgage but at least the guarantee of it opened the way for us to start bidding.

Shirley had only seen pictures of the property but had heard both mine and Tove's excitement. After asking valid and reasonable questions, she was on board — committing once again to a house she'd never been inside.

It was a Friday afternoon back in Northern Ireland. We made our first bid and within a few minutes an email informed us that another person had offered a slightly higher price. We bid again, and shortly afterwards, so did he. This continued for a couple of hours. Each time we made an offer, the other person bid slightly more within a short space of time.

Approaching our limit, we felt tense but reluctant to give up. We took the weekend to pray more about what our strategy should be, coming to the conclusion that God wanted us to make one last offer. This would be a larger amount than previously. We were convinced that we should be the next owners of the house and needed to state it firmly. This was taking me way out of my comfort zone but the bid was still just affordable — as long as we could get a reasonable price on the sale of our Irish home.

Come Monday morning, I pressed the button on our computer to register the final bid. Now we just had to wait for a phone call. "Congratulations, you've just bought a house in Sweden!" Marika said when she rang half an hour later. She went on to explain that the other bidder had pulled out. There was now no turning back — the house was ours. At the start of the process, Marika had been mystified as to how we could possibly want to buy a property in another country that one of us had not even seen inside. Now it appeared as if she understood too that there was a higher dimension to it all.

The next stage was an immediate transfer of the ten percent deposit. Thinking this was straightforward, I attempted to do it online. Even though the funds were in our bank account, the money just wouldn't go. We were about to leave for YWAM in the Faroe Islands so I advised

Marika that I'd put the transfer on hold. She didn't mind as long as the delay wasn't going to be too long.

On the plane, I browsed the inflight magazine. An advert for a money transfer service caught my eye. It seemed to be legitimate and was licensed in London. On reaching our destination, I researched it in depth. This service offered the transfer from our UK bank account to Sweden at a rate which, once more, saved us hundreds of pounds. Had God intervened to stop the first transfer going ahead — giving us time to find a better alternative? We are inclined to believe that He had.

From the Faroe's we went to Restenäs where Shirley was to teach in a YWAM school. We were finally able to see inside the house we had bought. In addition, we learned that someone in Restenäs would be moving shortly to YWAM near London. They were renting a trailer to take some furniture to their new location which would be returning empty. If we could get some of our things across from Ireland to London in time, then we could use that space free of charge. Appreciative of their offer, and thankful for yet more perfect timing, we found a way to make it work.

With Shirley's week of teaching over, we returned to Ireland in early November and contacted the estate agent who had sold us our home four years earlier.

"The market isn't great," he told us with a serious look when he came to do the valuation. "We can sell your home," then pausing before giving the bad news, "but only for less than you bought it for." That wasn't what we wanted to hear but there was no other option except to sell for what we could get. We were committed to going ahead in Sweden where the seller wanted us to complete their sale in early January.

Time was short, but we received a reasonable offer within a fortnight of advertising our house. Needing to get on with the process, we accepted and sent out a newsletter to our supporters telling them the good news. Only a couple of days later, the buyers came back insisting that they wanted to move in by Christmas, now only four weeks away. "How can we possibly get out so soon — and where would we go?" I asked Shirley. "We can't" was the terse reply and I knew that we were going to lose the sale.

There were no new enquiries about the house before Christmas. Concern was rising. If we couldn't sell in time to raise the funds needed for Restenäs, where would the money come from? The Swedish bank had made an eighty percent guarantee of the opening bid in their mortgage offer so we had that, but there was still going to be a short-fall. Catherine and her Korean husband HyeWon were due to visit from Seoul for the holidays; we tried to put our concerns aside to enjoy the festivities together.

Once Christmas was behind us, I emailed an updated newsletter on New Year's Day. Completion in Sweden was only nine days away so I wrote about the situation we'd found ourselves in, requesting prayer that God would have a creative solution for us. And of course, He did.

Later the same day, I drove Catherine and HyeWon to the airport for their return to Korea. Afterwards, still sad at saying "goodbye" and wondering when we'd see each other again, I stopped to fill up the car with fuel. Standing at the pump, my phone buzzed to indicate a text. Thinking it was a standard message advising the roaming cost for the Irish Republic, I almost ignored it.

Instead, the text was from friends of many years standing. They wanted to offer a significant interest-free loan for as long as we needed. It was to help us through the imminent crunch we were facing. God had used his people again to bless us. We took out the Swedish mortgage for the short-term too — the combined effect of this plus the loan, enabled us to pay for our new house on time.

In spite of assurances from the couple lending us the funds that there was no hurry to repay, we still hoped to be in a position to release the money from our Irish home as soon as we could. Time dragged on but still no serious offers were forthcoming. We had to get on with our move to Restenäs since we were committed to starting work there in March. In the end, someone who'd made an offer that was far too low to even consider, decided that they would increase their price to one we would be more open to accepting — although it was still lower than our original purchasing price.

Once more, Shirley and I processed and prayed. It was hard to give away a part of our investment to strangers.

Nevertheless, we had a strong impression that God wanted to teach us through the situation. We realised He was saying that He provides according to the need at the time and it isn't always about making profits. He had led us into that home in the first place. It had given a wonderful roof over our heads for the season which was coming to an end. We asked ourselves, "Are we willing to continue trusting Him even if we can't save any extra funds for future rainy days?" The Lord's Prayer reminds us to ask for bread on *this* day, to trust Him for the needs of the moment. We don't usually expect to make a profit when we sell things like cars or washing machines; how had we got into the mind-set that we *had* to when selling a house?

On the day we drove away from Ireland for our new life in Scandinavia, we knew that we were to accept the offer, doing so with real joy and peace in our hearts that things were falling into place. Even though we got a lower price than we'd hoped for, there was still enough to pay back our friends and the bank in Sweden too.

A few weeks after returning from their Christmas visit to Ireland, we'd had a Skype call with Catherine in Korea. Unable to contain her excitement, she announced, "You're going to become grandparents!" Then, without pausing for breath, she showed us a photo of a scan. "Here is number one baby." She quickly followed with a second picture, "This is number two, who is smaller. Your twin grand-children will be born in the summer." The babies were subsequently identified as two boys.

By the time we moved, Catherine had reached the second trimester of her pregnancy. But she still experienced severe sickness all day long, could hardly eat and was beginning to lose weight. She had no choice but to give up teaching English. The young couple decided to come to live with us in Sweden for a while so that we could help them. The home we'd just bought was big enough to accommodate them both plus our grandsons once they were born.

The Swedish healthcare system took great care of Catherine and her babies. The smaller of the two lads caused some concern as he was not gaining much weight. Regular check-ups were arranged, but before she had been to many of them, she started to go into labour at around twenty-six weeks. There was no hospital anywhere close to us which had the capacity to deal with premature twins. Phone calls were made and arrangements quickly put in place for Catherine to be flown by helicopter to a neonatal unit in Stockholm — on the other side of the country. Considered to be the best hospital in Sweden, they managed to prevent the labour progressing.

The regular checks continued while Catherine was on complete bedrest. The family of a YWAM colleague who lived a short distance from the hospital gladly opened their doors to HyeWon and to Shirley, who had gone over to support Catherine. About a week after moving to Stockholm, the smaller boy's weight in the womb was measured at 497 grams which probably would not have made him viable if he had been born too soon. His larger brother weighed in at around a kilogram at the same time.

Facebook can be very useful so we put out a prayer request asking for people to intercede for the lives of both of our grandsons. The news spread like wildfire. We later heard about people we've never met who joined in the prayer effort. The prayers of literally hundreds of people all over the world were answered. In less than a fortnight the smaller boy put on an additional fifty percent of his weight, with the bigger one gaining too. This was important as there were still concerns that they would be born prematurely. Friends started to pray that the twins would stay put until the smaller one had reached at least one kilogram.

The strain was showing on both Catherine and HyeWon so they asked to be moved to our side of Sweden. A room had become available in the hospital closest to our home so arrangements were made to fly them back. The timing was crucial. Two days later, Shirley and I were sitting in a YWAM meeting when HyeWon rang. "They're going to deliver the boys within the hour," he panted — breathless with anxiety. "Please come as soon as you can."

At thirty weeks' gestation on a gloriously sunny June afternoon, Catherine had an emergency C-section and our beautiful grandsons cried their way into life one minute apart. The larger one was named Alexander (meaning "great"). He weighed 1.52 kg at birth. He was followed by

Aidan ("fire") who had made it over the one-kilogram bar by coming in at 1.03 kg.

The boys were released from hospital at under six weeks old and came to stay with us. Amy quickly took to being an auntie and a new generation became part of our family. It had been quite a year! We had only just started to think about relocating to Sweden twelve months earlier. Now we were grandparents, we lived in Scandinavia and Amy was more fulfilled than ever. Our lives had taken on a complete change of focus and direction at an age when we were expected to start thinking of preparing for retirement.

Shirley and I cannot know what the future holds but we are convinced that God will be with us each step of the way. When we heard the call in Hawai'i all those years ago, we never could have imagined how our lives would have mapped out. We may lack the security of a regular salary from British Rail but our "Employer" has ensured that, in order to fulfil His calling on us, we have never been without anything we've needed.

"LORD, you alone are my portion and my cup; you have made my lot secure. The boundary lines have fallen for me in pleasant places; surely I have a delightful inheritance. I will praise the LORD, who counsels me; even at night my heart instructs me. . . . You have made known to me the path of life; you will fill me with joy in your presence, with eternal pleasures at your right hand." Psalm 16:5-7, 11.

Thank You, Lord, for Your incredible faithfulness and creative provision for our family during more than twenty years in Youth With A Mission. You truly are Jehovah Jireh, the God who provides. Our hope for the future is in You — the One who has proved trustworthy beyond any doubt.

Oh Dieu tu es mon Dieu, et je veux toujours te louer.
Je te chercherai dès l'aurore, j'apprendrai à marcher dans tes voies,
et pas à pas tu me conduis. C'est toi que je suivrai toute ma vie.

Oh God you are my God, and I will ever praise you.
I will seek you in the morning, I will learn to walk in your ways,
Step by step you lead me, and I will follow you all my days.

Postscript
BY PETER JORDAN

Missions today has many flavours, settings and out-workings. Unlike the typical image projected 100 years ago . . . of a man dressed in khakis and pith helmet, Bible in one hand and machete in the other, slashing his way through dense bush to reach some remote village in darkest Africa . . . missions today has evolved into a vastly broader picture.

What wasn't really portrayed back then was that meals had to be prepared, children cared for, finances managed plus a host of other details that came with living in a foreign country.

Today, the scope of missions and its related activities has broadened enormously. Almost any skill known to man can be employed in taking the Good News of Jesus Christ to the nations of the world.

Roy and Shirley have demonstrated that their individual giftings (administration, discipling, encouraging and

119

more), released under the call of God, can be just as effective in God's overall plan of reaching the nations, as the man in the pith helmet. Their story — though each person's is unique — is quite typical and easily applied to any Believer who is willing to obey God with their life. And then step out if called. The Jones Family did.

Peter Jordan, co-founder of YWAM
Associates International.

Appendix I

PURPOSE AND OUTCOMES OF A YWAM
DISCIPLESHIP TRAINING SCHOOL

1. To GATHER and CHALLENGE people to worship, listen to and obey God, releasing them (in the context of the DTS) to serve through evangelism, intercession, acts of compassion and other expressions of God's heart for the world, possibly even pioneering new ministries.

2. To **INSPIRE** and **CULTIVATE** growth in one's relationship with God resulting in Christ-like character, which is based on a solid Biblical foundation, the work of the Holy Spirit and the personal application of Biblical truth, especially concerning God's Character, the Cross and empowering Grace.

3. To **SHARPEN** one's ability to relate to, learn from and work with people, including those of different cultures, personalities and perspectives.

4. To further **EQUIP** each one to serve God's purposes either in or outside of the YWAM Family of Ministries, strengthening a commitment to reach the lost, especially the unreached, to care for the poor, and to influence all areas of society.

5. To **IMPART** the vision and foundational values of Youth With A Mission International as well as that of the host operating location and to provide information regarding a variety of opportunities for service.

The DTS aims to graduate students . . .

- with a growing understanding of the breadth and depth of God's character and ways
- who are becoming more like Jesus in the way they relate to God and people
- who increasingly cooperate with the empowering presence of the indwelling Holy Spirit
- who listen to and obey God as the result of God's enabling Grace
- who search the Scripture in such a way that transforms beliefs, values and behaviours
- with strengthened lifestyles of worship, intercession and spiritual warfare
- with a greater ability to work with others, especially those different to themselves
- who can share the Gospel with the lost and have a lifelong commitment to do so

- with a commitment to continue to be involved in some way with God's work among the nations, including unreached people, the poor and needy and in various spheres of society
- who understand the calling and values of YWAM and are aware of a variety of opportunities available to them throughout YWAM
- with a clearer understanding of God's purposes for their life and a sense of their life direction
- who either:
- go on to serve God in either a context familiar or foreign to them *or*
- pursue further training (in or outside of YWAM) to equip them for further service.

Appendix II

A FEW HIGHLIGHTS FROM OUR YWAM TIMELINE
(SO FAR)

August 1993: Holiday in Kona where God calls us into YWAM.

November 1993: Visit to Lausanne — only to discover that the YWAM centre is closed.

March 1994: Amy's heart surgery.

September 1994: We meet Loren Cunningham for the first time at YWAM Lausanne.

April 1995: Roy made redundant by British Rail.

June 1995: We start our Crossroads DTS in Salem, USA.

September 1995: Outreach to Romania.

July 1996: Roy works at Olympic Outreach in Atlanta.

January 1997: We leave Crondall for our new life in Lausanne.

September 1997: Shirley in Korea for University of the Nations workshop.

March 1998: Roy goes with Loren to Central America.

July 1998: Our first visit to Restenäs where we attend inTouch before going on to Latvia.

September 1998: Shirley staffs her first school in YWAM — a DTS in Lausanne followed by outreach to Amsterdam.

January 2000: Twelve-week Leadership Training School in Norway.

July 2002: Shirley and Catherine on outreach together in Togo, W. Africa.

August 2002: We co-lead our first inTouch Gathering in Switzerland.

August 2003: We move to Montcherand.

July 2005: We're commissioned as coordinators for YWAM-inTouch Europe.

August 2006: inTouch Europe starts to multiply, the first camp in France.

July 2007: Catherine in China with King's Kids.

March 2009: inTouch Jerusalem.

May 2010: First inTouch in Germany at Hurlach Castle.

October 2010: Leaving Switzerland, we move to YWAM Rostrevor, Northern Ireland.

January 2011: Catherine returns to Kona to take her own DTS followed by outreach in Macau.

July 2011: Shirley and Catherine together in Macau.

March 2012:	Shirley appointed to the Leadership Team of YWAM'S global university.
October 2013:	Roy in Kosovo and Bosnia for YWAM.
July 2014:	Shirley in New Zealand helping to edit the YWAM 'Sphere-view Bible'.
October 2014:	With YWAM in the Faroe Islands, including Roy on local radio.
March 2015:	We relocate to YWAM Restenäs.
May 2015:	Roy appointed an Elder for YWAM Central Europe Region.
June 2015:	Our twin grandsons born in Sweden.